The BreakThrough Series

SMALL BOOKS

A Life God
REWARDS

BRUCE WILKINSON
with DAVID KOPP

Multnomah®Publishers *Sisters, Oregon*

A LIFE GOD REWARDS
published by Multnomah Publishers, Inc.

© 2002 by Exponential, Inc.
International Standard Book Number: 1-57673-976-7

Cover design by David Carlson Design

Italics in Scripture quotations are the author's emphasis.

Scripture is from *The Holy Bible,* New King James Version.
Copyright © 1982 by Thomas Nelson, Inc. Used by permission.

Other Scripture quotations:
The Holy Bible, New International Version (NIV)
© 1973, 1984 by International Bible Society,
used by permission of Zondervan Publishing House

Multnomah is a trademark of Multnomah Publishers, Inc.,
and is registered in the U.S. Patent and Trademark Office.
The colophon is a trademark of Multnomah Publishers, Inc.

Printed in the United States of America

ALL RIGHTS RESERVED
No part of this publication may be reproduced, stored in a retrieval system,
or transmitted, in any form or by any means—electronic, mechanical, photocopying,
recording, or otherwise—without prior written permission.

For information:
MULTNOMAH PUBLISHERS, INC. • P.O. BOX 1720 • SISTERS, OR 97759

Library of Congress Cataloging-in-Publication Data:

Wilkinson, Bruce.
  A life god rewards / by Bruce Wilkinson.
     p. cm.
  ISBN 1-57673-976-7
  1. Future life—Christianity.   I. Title.
BT903 .W55 2002
236'.2—dc21

2002009394

02 03 04 05 06 07 08—10 9 8 7 6 5 4 3 2 1 0

Table of Contents

Acknowledgments 4

Preface 5

1. Keyhole to the Stars 7
2. The Unbreakable Link 18
3. What the Bible Says about Rewards 30
4. That Day 44
5. The Question of Your Life 60
6. The God Who Gives Back 76
7. The First Key 90
8. Seeing through to Forever 106

Christian Leaders on Eternal Rewards 118

Notes 124

*For those who might be wondering
today if God notices or cares.*

*I'm especially grateful to Don Jacobson for his
personal commitment to this project from its inception.
My thanks also to the whole Multnomah team,
especially to Jennifer Gott, Steffany Woolsey,
Bill Jensen, and Guy Coleman for their outstanding
support. And as always to my writing partner, David
Kopp, and our editor, Heather Harpham Kopp,
my deepest appreciation and respect.*

Preface

Dear Reader,

You're about to encounter the teachings of Jesus on a very surprising subject—the direct connection between what you do today and what you will experience in eternity.

Jesus revealed that two truths determine our eternal experience. Think of them as keys. The first key is belief—what you believe determines your eternal destination.

But what is the second key? What treasure from God does it unlock? And why did Jesus talk so much about it?

That is the subject of this book.

Jesus is recognized around the world and in every religion as a great teacher. Yet millions of people today, including a majority of His followers, do not seem to have heard what He said about a life God rewards. Have you?

The message of this little book has the potential to transform what you expect from God and what you will deeply desire to do for Him, starting today. I hope you read it prayerfully and expectantly.

Warmly,
Bruce Wilkinson

1

KEYHOLE TO THE STARS

"Rejoice in that day and leap for joy!
For indeed your reward is great in heaven."

JESUS, IN LUKE 6:23

What if today really *was* the first day of the rest of your life? Today you make your trade—everything you have accomplished and become for whatever God offers in exchange. There you are, poised on the brink, lifetime in hand, ready to step into eternity.

What a moment! And what an amazing exchange! Your blink in the sun for God's endless day. Your spoonful of water for His Amazon River.

You take your step. You put down your little handful of time and pick up your forever life....

> *No one made more shocking statements about the afterlife than Jesus.*

But what if I told you that the small choices you make today—like how you interact with your boss, or whom you invite to dinner—could change what happens next?

Would you be surprised?

In the little book you're holding, you're going to discover that Jesus revealed that our actions now will affect our future forever. Astoundingly, millions who follow Jesus seem to have missed what He said.

Could you be one?

I was. I grew up in a family that attended church regularly, and I was taught the Bible from the time I was young. Later I spent nine years pursuing theological training. But the clear teachings of Jesus on this subject remained lost to me, like overlooked treasures in my own house. When I finally discovered them, many things started to make sense for the first time.

Let's admit it: Any change in how we think about our future, even if it could radically improve our prospects, takes courage. We struggle to let go of comfortable assumptions, even when they're preventing us from seeing the whole truth. We're like toddlers peering through a keyhole at the night sky, trying to hold on to our tiny patch of stars.

But the keyhole is so small and the view is so great. Jesus wants to open the door and show us more.

Much more.

Prepare to Be Astonished

No one made more shocking statements about the afterlife than Jesus of Nazareth. His teachings often left His audiences amazed, dumbfounded, even outraged. Take His first public appearance at the age of twelve: "All who heard Him were astonished at His understanding and answers" (Luke 2:47).

When Jesus formally began His ministry, His audience was again "astonished" (Matthew 7:28). In His teaching known as the Sermon on the Mount, Jesus said:

> *"Blessed are you when men hate you,*
> *And when they exclude you,*
> *And revile you, and cast out your name as evil,*
> *For the Son of Man's sake.*
> *Rejoice in that day and leap for joy!"*
>
> LUKE 6:22–23

You might know these verses well. I have to confess that I read them dozens, if not scores, of times before I *really* read them. Jesus' statement seems incredible, doesn't it? I used to think He was saying something like, "If you are persecuted on My behalf, you'll be so happy that you'll jump for sheer delight."

But if you read on, it's clear that that's not what Jesus meant. He continued:

"For indeed your reward is great in heaven."

v. 23

In those eight words, Jesus reveals why you and I can rejoice, even in the worst circumstances. Why? Because there is a direct connection between something you do for Him on earth and something "great" He will do for you in heaven.

Notice that Jesus describes it as a reward for *doing*, which would distinguish it, for example, from a gift you receive for *believing*. Also, the reward is specifically and personally yours if you behave in one way, but is not yours if you behave in another (for example, if you ran away under the pressure of persecution).

You see, Jesus *isn't* asking you and me to enjoy misery on His behalf. Instead He's saying that the consequences in heaven for certain actions on earth will be so wonderful that simply knowing they're coming—and knowing that they will be great—can transform how we live now. Yes, and even create spontaneous outbursts of joy!

This promise of reward in heaven isn't an isolated example of Jesus' teachings on the subject:

- "He will *reward* each according to his works" (Matthew 16:27).
- "You will have *treasure* in heaven" (Matthew 19:21).
- "You will be blessed...for you shall be *repaid* at the resurrection" (Luke 14:14).

As you're about to discover, the implications of these passages are enormous. For one thing, they suggest that God is keeping track of what you do for Him every day. For another, that you have more to gain by serving Him than you ever imagined.

Tracking Down the Promise

Let me tell you how I came to write this book. In 1985 when I first stumbled upon Jesus' teachings on reward in heaven, I was startled. What He was saying seemed to contradict much of what I had always been taught and believed.

So I began an intensive search for the truth, starting with every Bible verse on the subject of eternal rewards. I studied theological and scholarly works. I spent hours thinking about what Jesus seemed to be saying with such urgency. And I became convinced that spiritual seekers around the world, including millions of Jesus' followers, had mislaid a truth of great importance and promise—and it was time to get it back.

Five years of in-depth study and twelve thick binders later, my findings lined the shelves of my study.

One day I got a call from Dr. Earl Radmacher, president of Western Seminary in Oregon, inviting me to present my material in a weeklong graduate course at the seminary. I agreed, but only after he promised to assemble a panel of leading scholars, including some who had also been studying rewards, to sit in and evaluate every word.

On an April morning several months later, I walked across the seminary campus, lugging my teaching materials. I arrived at the lecture room, which was filled with some of the brightest individuals I had ever met: department chairpersons of the Greek and Hebrew languages, church historians, Bible teachers, seminarians, and pastors from a range of denominations.

I taught every morning for four hours. Each afternoon, a special group of scholars met at Dr. Radmacher's home and debated every point.

What Jesus was saying seemed to contradict much of what I had always believed.

One day a church historian from Romania assured us that what we were studying was not new theology; it had been part of Christian beliefs and teaching from the first century on. To make his point he asked us, "What do the greats of church history such as Augustine, Luther, Calvin, Wesley, and Spurgeon all have in common?"

When everyone hesitated, he told us his answer: "They all earnestly believed in and hoped for eternal rewards."

Toward the end of the week, I noticed a shift. The roomful of scholars was spending less time debating and more time responding personally to the material. One afternoon an older participant pulled me aside. "I thought God brought me here to learn more about eternal rewards," he said, "but I was wrong. He brought me here to change my heart—I'm leaving a changed professor!"

We'll carefully construct the biggest, truest view posssible of your entire life.

On the last day, I asked the group, "Are you convinced that what I've been teaching about rewards is consistent with what Jesus taught?"

"We're convinced," they replied. And I have never looked back.

The Two Keys

In the pages ahead, you'll encounter for yourself the findings we explored that week at Western Seminary. Whether you're familiar with Jesus' teachings about eternal rewards or you're coming upon them for the first time, I encourage you to read with great expectation. Important spiritual breakthroughs await you.

Starting with statements Jesus made, we'll carefully construct the biggest, truest view possible of your entire life. We'll be using a lot of familiar words—words like *heaven, treasure, works,* and *faith.* I urge you to be patient as we look beneath these familiar labels for hidden insights.

The teachings of Jesus show us that there are two keys that determine everything about your eternity.

The first key is your *belief.* This key unlocks the door to eternal life and determines *where* you will spend eternity.

The second key is your *behavior.* It unlocks the door to reward and determines *how* you will spend eternity.

This second key is the focus of *A Life God Rewards.* Although the role of behavior (we'll also use words like *actions* or *works*) isn't more important to your future than belief, it has been more overlooked in recent times. And the promise of rediscovering the truths it unlocks is enormous, especially for followers of Jesus.

In fact, by the time you're done reading, you'll

approach daily life in a dramatically different way. Simple decisions, such as how you spend your time and money, will become opportunities of great promise. And you will begin to live with an unshakable certainty that everything you do today matters forever.

Rumors of Blue Whales

In the first book in this series, *The Prayer of Jabez,* we learned that God wants us to ask for His blessing and for greater influence, or "territory," in this world. The next book, *Secrets of the Vine,* showed that Jesus wants our territory to produce a great harvest of good works for Him.

In *A Life God Rewards,* I want to show you how the harvest you produce will directly impact your experience in eternity—and how that truth can change your life today for the better.

I'll admit that on a subject like eternity, we must proceed thoughtfully and humbly. We're

You will begin to live with an unshakable certainty that everything you do today matters forever.

like tadpoles swapping stories of blue whales. We're like one twin in the womb trying to convince his brother that it's only a matter of time before they're both breathing air and riding tricycles.

Fortunately for all of us, God sent His Son from heaven to help us see the whole truth. If you and I are willing to be surprised, unsettled, even shocked by His words, our prospects for living a life He rewards will change for the better, starting now.

2

THE UNBREAKABLE LINK

"For the Son of Man will come in the glory of His Father with His angels, and then He will reward each according to his works."

JESUS, IN MATTHEW 16:27

Blink.

That's the first thing you'll notice—simply no transition. No bridge from temporary to eternal. No gradual awakening. No strolling toward heaven through a long corridor of light (where you might, for example, rethink your direction and decide to go back). No spare moment to decide that, yes, it finally is time to consider what God said.

You will go from instant to instant. One instant, earth; the next, eternity....

Blink.

The Unbreakable Link

And then what?

If you're like most people, you picture eternity somewhat like a West Texas highway—flat, long, and monotonous. You expect that after your death all the big events of your life will be behind you.

But Jesus reveals something else entirely. As the only person to come from eternity to earth, then return to eternity, Jesus knows the whole truth—past, present, and future—and can give you a one-of-a-kind perspective. For example, He can see your present (there you are, reading *A Life God Rewards*) from a moment far out in your infinite future and tell you exactly how to prepare for what is to come.

Most people picture eternity somewhat like a West Texas highway—flat, long, and monotonous.

Listen to a moment in the future that Jesus told His disciples about:

> *"For the Son of Man will come in the glory of His Father with His angels, and then He will reward each according to his works."*
>
> MATTHEW 16:27

Jesus was describing a specific series of events in every believer's future that will alter our experience of eternity: He will come again, He will bring rewards, and His rewards will be given to "each according to his works." Since Jesus hasn't yet come again, we can conclude that even His disciples are still waiting in heaven for the event Jesus described in this verse.

Does this news surprise you?

If so, you will appreciate what comes next. To help you get the most out of what Jesus wants you to know about His rewards, we're going to start with the big picture first. In this chapter, we'll step back from the keyhole, let Jesus open the door, and get a big Milky Way view of every person's future.

And you'll understand how the long line of your future is being decided by one little dot called today.

THE (REAL) TIMELINE OF YOUR ETERNITY

If we look closely at what Jesus said, we discover that our eternal life has a clear and knowable timeline of events. In fact, Jesus revealed that most of our life happens *after* our physical death.

The timeline that follows focuses on events that

will happen to you in the future. Jesus talked about these events often. And they apply to you no matter what your religion or what choices you're making today about your beliefs or actions.

We'll get more details later, but for now, think of the timeline as a road map to your future with only the main intersections marked.

THE SIX MAIN EVENTS OF YOUR FOREVER LIFE

1. LIFE. *You are created in the image of God for a life of purpose.*

Let's start with now. Although you didn't exist forever in the past, you will continue to exist forever in the future. Between birth and death, you live on earth as a body, soul, and spirit (John 3:6; 4:23–24; 1 Thessalonians 5:23).

2. DEATH. *You die physically, but not spiritually.*

Just as birth is your brief entrance into life on earth, so the death of your body is your instantaneous exit. Yet since you are more than organic matter, your life as soul and spirit continues. Neither reincarnation nor "soul sleep" is taught in the Bible. Jesus revealed that after death your soul is either with God in heaven or apart from God in hell (Luke 23:43; 2 Corinthians 5:8).

3. DESTINATION. *You reach your destination after death, which is determined by what you believed on earth.*

Your eternal destination is decided by whether you believed in Jesus while you were still alive (John 3:16–18). In all of His teaching, Jesus identified only two possible locations in the afterlife: heaven or hell (John 14:2; Matthew 23:33). Both last forever.

4. RESURRECTION. *You receive a resurrected body.*

In eternity, every person will experience bodily resurrection (John 5:28–29). Our new bodies will be immortal—they can never again experience death (1 Corinthians 15). For those who are resurrected to life, Jesus "will transform our lowly body that it may be conformed to His glorious body" (Philippians 3:21).

5. REPAYMENT. *You receive your reward or your retribution for eternity based on what you did on earth.*

Although your eternal destination is based on your belief, how you spend eternity is based on your behavior while on earth. Believers and nonbelievers will be judged by Jesus Christ at events called the bema and the great white throne (John 5:22; 2 Corinthians 5:10; Revelation 20:11–15). The outcome will determine your degree of reward in heaven or retribution in hell (Matthew 11:21–22; 23:14).

6. ETERNITY. *You will live forever in the presence or absence of God, reaping the consequences of your beliefs and actions on earth.*

Jesus taught that an eternal existence awaits everyone. Those who have rejected Him "will go away into everlasting punishment," while those who have chosen Him will experience eternal life in God's presence (Matthew 25:46). The eternity that Jesus reveals is not just an existence or state of mind, but a real life in a real place.

If you're already familiar with what the Bible says about future events, you may have noticed that some were not included, such as the Rapture, the Second Coming of Jesus, the Tribulation, and the Kingdom. That's because we've tried to describe a broad view of the events everyone will experience.

Make the Connection

Even a whirlwind tour of eternity shows just how much is at stake in what lies ahead for you. Clearly your future according to Jesus holds great promise for fulfillment and reward—if you make certain choices now.

Which brings us to a connection that many miss. Maybe you've already seen it.

If you look at the six main events of your forever life in terms of cause and effect, you'll notice that your life now is directly impacting everything that will happen to you after you die. Between your life on earth and every later event in your life, there is an invisible, one-way connection.

I describe this critical connection as the Law of the Unbreakable Link:

The Unbreakable Link

Your choices on earth have direct consequences on your life in eternity.

Think of the Law of the Unbreakable Link like the law of gravity—it's always present, always working, even when you can't see it and even if you don't believe it. The choices you make in your life don't come to nothing when you die. They matter. And they will continue to matter throughout eternity!

Your future holds great promise for fulfillment and reward— if you make certain choices now.

When we study the events of our timeline, we see that there are really two sets of consequences (I described them as keys in chapter 1):

- Our eternal destination is the consequence of what we believe on earth.
- Our eternal compensation is the consequence of how we behave on earth.

I grew up understanding only part of what the link shows. I knew that what I believed on earth would affect where I spent eternity. But I assumed that my actions (once the issue of my belief was resolved) would not have a direct consequence on what heaven would be like for me. You can see that I applied the link to my faith but not to my actions.

Let me ask you, do you believe your choices today *are* directly linked to what you will experience in your eternity?

It's been my observation that people all over the world fall into one of two camps on this issue. One camp emphasizes the consequence of beliefs on an individual's eternal future and tends to minimize the importance of works. The other camp emphasizes the consequence of good works on an individual's eternal future and tends to minimize the issue of belief.

Each camp tends to look down on the other—and, unfortunately, sees only part of the big picture.

Jesus came to show you how you can change your future, beginning with one small choice.

Do these observations ring true in your experience?

And let me ask you: Which consequence of the link may have slipped from view in your thinking?

Consider what rediscovering the connection between your life now and your life in eternity could mean for you. If your actions today *do* have the potential to radically affect your eternity, wouldn't that dramatically change how you think about your life? How you think about God? What you choose to do one minute from now?

Jesus wants you to know that the positive consequences of your actions and beliefs today can change your eternity in astounding and wonderful ways—and He doesn't want you to waste another minute believing otherwise.

You don't need to wonder or worry about what might await you on the other side of your last heartbeat. In His great mercy, Jesus came to earth from eternity so you could know exactly what consequences your actions and beliefs will have there.

And because He came, eternity need hold no threat, only great promise.

The Dot and the Line

I want to show you a picture that will help you keep the reality of the unbreakable link at the forefront of your thinking as you make your daily choices.

Below you see a dot and a line. The dot is small and exists in one little place. The line begins in one place, then takes off across the page. Imagine that the line extends off the page and goes on and on, without end.

The dot stands for your whole life here on earth. For most of us, that's about seventy years.

The line represents your life after death in eternity. That's forever and ever.

As we saw in our timeline, Jesus' teaching shows that *what happens inside the dot determines everything that happens on the line.* Even a small choice in the dot can result in a corresponding consequence on the line of astounding proportions.

Whenever audiences grasp this mental picture, their reactions are immediate and intense. They say things like, "If this is true, it changes everything for me!" Or, "I can't believe I've prepared for my children's future and my old age without giving a thought to my *real* future!" One man said to me, "I've always thought about finishing well, but it turns out that death is just the starting gate!"

You don't need to wonder or worry about what might await you on the other side of your last heartbeat.

Can you identify with any of these reactions? Would you say you've been living for the line or for the dot?

If your answer is the latter, your prospects are about to look up. Jesus came to show you how you can change your future, beginning with one small choice.

Just ask a group of dinner guests....

3

WHAT THE BIBLE SAYS ABOUT REWARDS

"When you give a feast, invite the poor, the maimed, the lame, the blind. And you will be blessed, because they cannot repay you; for you shall be repaid at the resurrection of the just."

JESUS, IN LUKE 14:13–14

It happened one Sabbath. Jesus, along with a distinguished list of guests, had been invited to dinner at the home of a prominent leader (Luke 14:1). As the guests were finding their places, Jesus watched them jockey for the best seats.

Suddenly, He offered some unsolicited advice:

"Sit down in the lowest place.... For whoever exalts himself will be humbled, and he who humbles himself will be exalted."

VV. 10–11

Everywhere, power players flinched. But Jesus wasn't finished. He turned to the host and proceeded to instruct him on a better way to entertain guests:

> *"When you give a dinner or a supper, do not ask your friends, your brothers, your relatives, nor rich neighbors, lest they also invite you back, and you be repaid."*
>
> V. 12

What an awkward moment! Jesus seemed to be saying to His host, "Next time, don't invite all these people you invited tonight."

Was He questioning the man's taste in friends or his grasp of social etiquette? Look closely at what Jesus said next:

> *"When you give a feast, invite the poor, the maimed, the lame, the blind. And you will be blessed."*
>
> VV. 13–14

Rather than criticizing His host for his generosity, Jesus was showing him how to get something

> *That evening, Jesus had something else in mind.*

important—something more lasting than a wonderful evening—in exchange for it. The first hint we get of that something is in the word *blessed*.

Blessed! All of us know that feeling. My family experienced it one day when we pulled off the highway for lunch and decided to buy a meal for a homeless traveler sitting outside the restaurant. When my daughter presented him with the biggest cheeseburger on the menu, he beamed at her with a toothless smile, and we made a new friend.

I still remember how I felt as our car pulled back onto the interstate. Completely rewarded. All-over warm. Yes, Jesus was right. Blessings do come when you do good deeds to those who cannot repay you.

But that's not what Jesus was talking about.

That evening, Jesus had something else in mind.

What Jesus Said Next

The rest of Jesus' statement brings us to the heart of the Bible's teaching on rewards:

"And you will be blessed, because they cannot repay you; for you shall be repaid at the resurrection of the just."

v. 14

No one in the room could have missed Jesus' astonishing revelation—God will repay you for a good work *after you are dead*. This contradicts what most people believe today and what everyone in that room believed—that God rewards people only on earth for the good they do in this life.

Jesus revealed just the opposite. His words show that when you do a worthy deed for a person who cannot repay you:

1. You will be repaid.
2. Your payment will come in the next life.
3. When you receive it, you will be blessed.

Certainly, God blesses us here on earth out of His unmerited grace and goodness. God may also give us temporal rewards for right choices or faithful service to Him in the here and now. But the rewards Jesus reveals in this story—and the ones He talks about most—are different. They are God's guaranteed response to a specific action on our part that will continue to affect our lives far into eternity. These rewards come not from asking, but from doing—and not now, but after death.

Miss these differences and you set yourself up for disappointment. You'll find yourself asking questions like these: *I serve God in every way I know how, so why is our family struggling so much financially? Doesn't God notice or care?* Friend, God notices and cares. But He doesn't promise that work for Him now will always result in gain from Him now.

In fact, the rewards Jesus wanted you and me to know about most do *not* come now. He said it in His first sermon, and He said it again to a roomful of religious know-it-alls at dinner....

His eternal rewards come later, and they begin with something you do today.

What Does Jesus Mean by *Reward*?

Interestingly, the Bible uses two different words to describe Jesus' reward.

What the Bible Says about Rewards

The Greek word used in Jesus' teachings in Luke 6 is *misthos*. Literally, it means *wages:* "Rejoice in that day and leap for joy! For indeed your *misthos* [wages] are great in heaven" (Luke 6:23).

Jesus used the same word later when He spoke of earthly wages: "Call the laborers and give them their *misthos* [wages]" (Matthew 20:8). And Paul told Timothy, "The laborer is worthy of his *misthos* [wages]" (1 Timothy 5:18).

Everyone who heard Jesus understood exactly what He meant: "When you labor on earth, your employer gives you *misthos*. And when you labor for Me, I pay you wages, too."

Jesus never described His reward as a charitable tip ("Here's a little something extra"), or a token of appreciation (like a plaque for thirty years at the factory). He called it wages—something you earn resulting from something you do.

The second word used for reward in heaven

Jesus' rewards begin with something you do today.

appears in our dinner story in this chapter. Here Jesus used a compound word, *apodidomai*. *Apo* means *back*, and *didomai* means *to give*. Combined, *apodidomai* means to give back in return, or simply, repay:

> "You will be blessed...for you shall be *apodidomai* [given back in return] at the resurrection of the just."
>
> LUKE 14:14

Jesus also used this term in His well-known story about the Good Samaritan, who stopped to help a traveler that had been beaten and robbed by bandits. When the Samaritan took the injured man to a nearby inn for care, he told the innkeeper, "Take care of him; and whatever more you spend, when I come again, I will *apodidomai* [repay] you" (Luke 10:35).

The word *apodidomai* takes the idea of wages into even more surprising territory. Jesus says that when you receive His *apodidomai*, you are being reimbursed in full measure for what you did on His behalf. If you're thinking that God would repay you only for grand acts of personal sacrifice and not everyday acts of love, remember that Jesus said, "For whoever gives you a cup of water to drink in My name...will by no means lose his *apodidomai* [repayment]" (Mark 9:41).

Have you heard and embraced Jesus' amazing promise? No deed for God will pass by overlooked or unrewarded. Not one cup of water, or one prayer in the middle of the night.

> *Jesus never described His reward as a charitable tip.*

PORTRAIT OF A LIFE

I visited recently with a bedridden elderly woman named Vera. "I get so discouraged lying here all day, Dr. Wilkinson," she said. "I can't really *do* anything for God but pray."

"Do you pray a lot?" I asked.

Vera thought for a minute before replying. "Oh, for half of my day, I suppose. And some of the night, too."

I encouraged Vera by reminding her that Jesus said private prayer is so valuable to God that "your Father who sees in secret will reward you openly" (Matthew 6:6).

Maybe, like Vera, you're doing more of eternal value than you realize. So what would a portrait of a life God rewards look like?

Nowhere does Jesus give an exhaustive list of what actions He will reward. Yet I've observed in cultures around the world that people know instinctively what a good work is—an act you do for someone that meets a need and honors God. In *Secrets of the Vine*, we saw how much God wants and works for this kind of fruitfulness in every person's life. Jesus told His disciples, "By this My Father is glorified, that you bear much fruit" (John 15:8).

We see a vivid picture of the life God rewards in the teachings of Jesus and in the rest of the New Testament. To help you remember this portrait of a life God rewards, I've used words beginning with *S*. Vera is a good example of the first *S*:

Maybe you're doing more of eternal value than you realize.

1. God will reward you for *seeking* Him through spiritual acts such as fasting and praying (Matthew 6:6; Hebrews 11:6).

2. God will reward you for *submitting* to your employer as a faithful steward (Matthew 24:45–47; Ephesians 6:8; Colossians 3:22–24).
3. God will reward you for *self-denial* in His service (Matthew 16:24–27).
4. God will reward you for *serving* those in need in His name (Mark 9:41).
5. God will reward you for *suffering* for His name and reputation (Luke 6:22–23).
6. God will reward you for *sacrifices* you make for Him (Luke 6:35). In fact, Jesus said that every person who sacrifices to follow Him will be rewarded a hundredfold (Matthew 19:29)!
7. God will reward you for *sharing* of your time, talent, and treasure to further His kingdom (Matthew 6:3–4; 1 Timothy 6:18–19).

As you read this list, you might see areas where you have already made a priority of doing what God promises to reward. Or you might read the list and feel discouraged: *This looks like the description of a supersaint like Billy Graham or Mother Teresa. How could someone like me possibly earn rewards?*

Let me reassure you. In the pages to come, you're going to see that every person on earth, regardless of circumstance or ability, has an equal opportunity to please God and receive His "Well done, good and faithful servant" (Matthew 25:21).

GOD'S PREROGATIVE

I've noticed that people who are making these discoveries for the first time respond with a wide range of feelings. Some experience intense gratitude; some, a burst of anticipation. But others tell me they are reluctant to believe what they're hearing. They'll say, "But I don't deserve any reward!" Or, "If I'm spending eternity with Jesus in heaven, why would I want or need anything more?"

I understand these feelings. I had them myself when I first explored this topic. In fact, I didn't agree with God's plan at all! I'd been happily working for God for years. I couldn't believe that God would want to reward

I couldn't believe that God would want to reward me for what I was already willingly doing for Him.

me for what I was already willingly doing for Him. After all, Jesus died for me. Serving Him was the least I could do for Him!

Two passages in the Gospels helped my thinking begin to change:

- In Luke 17:10, Jesus told His disciples: "When you have done all those things which you are commanded, say, 'We are unprofitable servants. We have done what was our duty to do.'"

This passage shows that, above all, it is my duty and privilege to serve God. If Jesus thanks me, it is because He is gracious and generous, not because I am deserving.

- In Matthew 20:1–16, Jesus told a parable about laborers who worked different lengths of time but all received the same wages. At the end of the day, when the workers who had worked all day questioned the landowner's fairness, he said, "Is it not lawful for me to do what I wish with my own things? Or is your eye evil because I am good?" (v. 15).

This second passage reminds me that God can be as generous as He wants with what belongs to Him. If I argue with His amazing goodness, it may be because goodness is lacking in my own heart.

Then one day I reencountered a familiar verse that changed my thinking on this matter once and for all.

MEET THE REWARDER

You'll find this verse in Hebrews, nestled in a passage about heroes who pleased God with their faith. "Without faith it is impossible to please Him," the writer says, "for he who comes to God must believe that He is, and that He is a *rewarder*" (11:6).

If you look up that word *rewarder* in the Greek, you'll be amazed by what you discover. The word used here is neither *misthos* nor *apodidomai*, but an unusual combination of both. In fact, Hebrews 11:6 is the only verse in the Bible where you'll find it used to describe a person. God is the *misthos-apodidomai*—the rewarder who pays back your wages in return.

You see, God chooses to reward because it is an expression of His own generous nature. His plan to reward, like His provision to save, is a display of His amazing grace.

And there's no other way to think about it. The Bible says if you want to please God, you *must* believe that "He is," but you also *must* believe something else. That your God "is a rewarder."

Today, this takes faith. But in the next chapter I'll take you to the day in your future when Jesus will prove it to you face-to-face.

"He who comes to God must believe that He… is a rewarder."

4

THAT DAY

"For the Father judges no one,

but has committed all judgment to the Son,

that all should honor the Son

just as they honor the Father."

JESUS, IN JOHN 5:22–23

Have you ever sat, eyes glued to the television, watching the Olympic awards ceremonies with tears streaming down your cheeks?

I have. There's something about the scene that pulls at a person's heart.

Your favorite athlete climbs the steps of the awards platform, her national anthem fills the stadium, her nation's flag waves in the spotlight. Her years of sweat and self-denial have paid off. She has finished her race. And she has won.

Now, as thousands applaud, an Olympic official drapes a medal around her neck.

One day you and I will have our own awards ceremony in eternity. The halls of heaven will ring with praise and celebration. Witnesses from every nation and every generation will watch with eager anticipation. Even angels will pause....

Because our race of faith will be done. The moment will have arrived for us to stand at the platform and receive our reward.

On that day, who do you think will be our judge and rewarder?

One day you and I will have our own awards ceremony in eternity.

The best judge would be a person who understands complete justice from heaven's perspective but who also knows what it feels like to live in the heat and dust and discouragement of everyday life.

Only Jesus could be the One. The Bible says He was "in all points tempted as we are, yet without sin" (Hebrews 4:15). And in fact, the Bible says Jesus *will* be our judge. Jesus Himself announced to His disciples that the authority to judge had been given to Him by God:

> *"For the Father judges no one, but has committed all judgment to the Son."*
>
> JOHN 5:22

Paul, thinking ahead to his own awards ceremony, wrote: "There is laid up for me the crown of righteousness, which the Lord, the righteous Judge, will give to me on that Day, and not to me only but also to all who have loved His appearing" (2 Timothy 4:8).

Do you look forward to meeting your Savior in person? Then this chapter is especially for you. We will look more deeply into Event 5: Repayment.

We'll begin by giving you a picture of what you will experience when you stand before Jesus to receive His repayment for what you did in your life on earth. Remember, everyone will give an account, and everyone will receive compensation from God based on his works. When the apostle Paul wrote to churches, he referred to a judgment at the bema of

Jesus. The apostle John wrote about a judgment at a great white throne.

In the next few minutes, we're going to answer some important questions about that wonderful occasion: How will Jesus evaluate what we did for Him? What could we gain or lose? And how will we respond?

No one wrote in more detail about that day than the apostle Paul, perhaps because he experienced an unexpected preview of its significance one day in the Greek city of Corinth....

Paul at the Bema

Paul had been living in Corinth for several months, spreading the news of the gospel at every opportunity, when trouble hit. His enemies dragged him into court and charged him with "persuading the people to worship God in ways contrary to the law" (Acts 18:13, NIV).

Scholars believe that a raised marble platform still visible today in the ruins of Corinth is the exact place where the provincial magistrate sat to hear Paul's case. The platform was called the *bema*, which is the Greek word for *judgment seat*. The same word was applied to the place where officials sat at athletic contests. The bema represented authority, justice, and reward (John 19:13; Acts 25:10–12).

At Paul's hearing, he stood before a magistrate named Gallio while his enemies argued for his punishment. But when it came Paul's turn to defend himself, Gallio stopped the proceedings. He had already decided that no crime had occurred. Paul was free to go.

Considering the apostle's tumultuous life, the incident at the bema in Corinth was a mere blip.

Or was it?

Three years later, Paul sent a letter back to the church in Corinth. In it he talked about another bema, this one in heaven. He told them that every follower of Jesus would have an appointment there one day:

For we must all appear before the judgment seat [bema] of Christ, that each one may receive the things done in the body, according to what he has done, whether good or bad.

2 CORINTHIANS 5:10

Notice two important phrases: When Paul writes "that each one may receive," he is clearly indicating a reward or repayment. And when he says "things done in the body," he is restricting the reward to things you did while you were alive on earth. As you know, this takes place in heaven after you die.

The scene that played out on the stones of Corinth gave Paul a compelling picture—one he wanted the church in Corinth to see and remember: We will all face the bema, we will all stand alone, and our judge will be Jesus Christ Himself.

SHOW AND TEST

Two years later, when Paul wrote to encourage the Christians in Rome, the bema came up again:

> *We shall all stand before the judgment seat [bema] of Christ.... Each of us shall give account of himself to God.*
>
> ROMANS 14:10, 12

What did Paul mean by "give account"? A different visual description of our judgment, found in 1 Corinthians 3, gives some key insights. In it, Paul pictures not a platform but a building, which represents our works, undergoing a test by fire:

Now if anyone builds on this foundation with gold, silver, precious stones, wood, hay, straw, each one's work will become clear; for the Day will declare it, because it will be revealed by fire.

VV. 12–13

You aren't being tested here. Your beliefs aren't being tested, either.

We know from the previous verse that the foundation Paul refers to is Jesus. When put together, these verses clarify that the first purpose of the bema is to *show*. Notice the key words—*become clear, declare,* and *revealed*. At a time of accounting after Jesus comes (Paul, like Jesus, calls it "the Day"), all that we have done for God will be plainly and completely apparent.

A second purpose of the judgment at the bema is to *test* our works:

The fire will test each one's work, of what sort it is. If anyone's work which he has built on it endures, he will receive a reward. If anyone's work is burned, he will suffer loss; but he himself will be saved, yet so as through fire.

VV. 13–15

Notice that *you* aren't being tested here. *Your beliefs* aren't being tested. And *your destination* in eternity isn't being tested.

So what is tested at the bema? *Your works.* What you did with your life will endure like gold, silver, and precious stones in a fire. Or it will burn up like straw—not a trace will remain, no matter how sensible, enjoyable, or even religious these activities might have seemed while you were alive.

To help you grasp the purpose of our "show and test" in heaven, picture two followers of Jesus approaching the bema. One is a high-ranking church leader, the other a street vendor. First one and then the other stands for judgment. Each in turn sees every work he did piled high on the altar. Then the pile is tested by fire.

Who of these two will step into eternity with the most reward?

The fire will make the truth obvious to all.

The answer is that before the fire of the bema, *we can't possibly know.* Until then, only God knows what any person's work for Him is worth. That's why Paul encouraged Christians to "judge nothing before the time, until the Lord comes.... Then each one's praise will come from God" (1 Corinthians 4:5).

Only after the test by fire will we finally see how a person's life has added up for eternity. The fire will make the truth obvious to all. And when we see it, we will completely agree with the judgment of Jesus and the reward or loss that follows.

THE GOLD STANDARD

By now you might be wondering what would cause a work to either burn like straw or endure like gold. Obviously the fire would need to test not only *what* we did, but also *how* and *why* we did it.

In the previous chapter, we painted a portrait to show what a life God rewards might look like. But Jesus said that genuine good behavior always begins in the heart (Luke 6:43–45).

Think of the three tests that follow—all gleaned from the teachings of Jesus—as the gold standard to help you evaluate whether the work you do for God will endure:

1. *The Test of Relationship.* It might relieve you to know that a life God rewards is not about performance apart from relationship with Jesus. In fact, just the opposite is true. Jesus said unless His followers stay close to Him and obey His commands, they will not bear "much fruit" for Him—"for without Me you can do nothing" (John 15:5).

    In the book of Revelation, Jesus commended the church at Ephesus for its many good works, but was grieved because they had not kept their love for Him alive. He said, "I know your works, your labor, your patience.... Nevertheless I have this against you, that you have left your first love" (2:2, 4).

2. *The Test of Motive.* Jesus said, "Take heed that you do not do your charitable deeds before men, to be seen by them. Otherwise you have no reward from

your Father in heaven" (Matthew 6:1). What should be our motive? To serve God and bring Him glory. Even ordinary actions like eating and drinking can bring God glory (1 Corinthians 10:31). By contrast, our most "religious" action is worthless if our motive is to build up our own egos or reputations.

3. *The Test of Love.* True good works are always focused on sincerely trying to improve the well-being of another. Jesus said, "But love your enemies, do good, and lend, hoping for nothing in return; and your reward will be great, and you will be sons of the Most High. For He is kind to the unthankful and evil" (Luke 6:35). In Paul's famous passage on love, he pointed out that without love, good deeds will not benefit the doer: "Though I bestow all my goods to feed the poor, and though I give my body to be burned, but have not love, it profits me nothing" (1 Corinthians 13:3).

While it's important to remember that everything we do for God will be judged at the bema, we don't have to be anxious that a work will fail the test of the bema because of something we never heard about.

Jesus will bring no criterion to the judgment that He hasn't clearly revealed in Scripture and empowered us to meet by His Spirit (2 Peter 1:2–4).

So what did Paul mean by the words *suffer loss?*

"How Could I 'Lose' in Heaven?"

The tested-by-fire passage in 1 Corinthians 3 ends with a very sobering prospect: "If anyone's work is burned, he will *suffer loss;* but he himself will be saved, yet so as through fire" (v. 15).

This is the part about our futures that so few believers I know have ever grasped: When we stand before the bema of Jesus, *we may suffer loss.*

What a startling thought! Is it possible that a true follower of Jesus—even though his or her salvation is not at risk at the bema—could step into eternity with few good works to show for his or her lifetime on earth?

Yes. That is exactly what could happen, according to these passages.

It seems clear from these passages that you could do a work and then lose the reward for it. No wonder the apostle John warned, "Look to yourselves, that we do not lose those things we worked for, but that we may receive a full reward" (2 John 1:8).

No wonder he pleaded, "Little children, abide in Him, that when He appears, we may have confidence and not be ashamed before Him at His coming" (1 John 2:28).

Still, the primary purpose of the bema is not loss, but gain. Even though the consequences of missed opportunities and lost reward will go with us into eternity, any regret or shame we might experience will not. How can I be sure? Because the Bible promises that "God will wipe away every tear from their eyes" (Revelation 21:4).

The amazing truth is that, regardless of what happens at the bema, Jesus will not love you any less or any more for all eternity than He loved you when He purchased your life with His own blood—or than He loves you right now as you're reading this book.

Let me leave you with one more surprise: Jesus wants you to keep it all.

Friend, join me in living wholeheartedly for a day of celebration, not disappointment, at the bema. No reward on earth will compare to the pleasure of seeing unclouded joy on the face of our Savior as He reviews the work of our lives, then leans forward to favor us with the reward He most wants to give.

A Reward to Keep

At that moment, when Jesus gives us the reward for our life, when we finally and completely see and understand all that God has done for us and in us and through us—and we know fully that without Him we could not have done even one commendable work for Him—our overwhelming response will be to cry out in thanks and praise to Him.

At that moment, out of sheer joy and gratitude, you'll want to fall in worship at the feet of the Lord Jesus Christ and give back everything He has just given to you. But let me leave you with one more surprise.

Jesus wants you to keep it all.

As we'll see in the next chapter, His plan is for you to enjoy and make good use of your rewards for the rest of eternity. The popular assumption that we will cast our crowns before Christ is based on a well-intentioned misreading of Revelation 4:10–11. There we see a specific group of elders worshiping God by casting their crowns at His feet. Yet the context shows that these elders do not represent all believers. And the verses show that their act of worship—casting their crowns—is repeated over and over throughout eternity.

Will you, like those awestruck worshipers, want to respond unreservedly to God once you see His amazing power and love? Absolutely!

But the *misthos* and *apodidomai* of Jesus are not momentary but *eternal* rewards—the everlasting consequence of your choice to serve Him during your brief time on earth, and the everlasting proof of His limitless love. One of the most dramatic pictures of rewards that last forever is seen in Daniel 12:3: "Those who are wise shall shine like the brightness of the firmament, and those who turn many to righteousness like the stars forever and ever."

And your rewards are meant to be yours eternally.

If you're thinking that as wonderful as they might be, you can't imagine needing or wanting more reward than heaven itself, you're in for a surprise! In the next two chapters, I'll show you from the words of Jesus that the rewards you receive in heaven will determine a lot about what you actually *do* there.

And what you will most want to do in heaven may be the greatest surprise of all.

5

THE QUESTION OF YOUR LIFE

"Whoever desires to become great among you shall be your servant.... For even the Son of Man did not come to be served, but to serve, and to give His life a ransom for many."

JESUS, IN MARK 10:43, 45

When you get there, what do you think your most powerful desire in heaven will be?

It took eighty thousand men to give me a clue.

I was part of a capacity crowd of Christian men gathered in Detroit's cavernous Silverdome stadium. When the speaker finished, the worship team stepped up to lead us in the hymn "Holy, Holy, Holy."

What started as a quiet refrain increased in volume with each verse. When we finished the hymn we started over, this time louder. Eventually the stadium seemed to shake—from the playing field to the highest tier—with the sound of our worship.

Holy, holy, holy! Lord God Almighty!
Early in the morning our song shall rise to Thee;
Holy, holy, holy!

We sang it on our knees. We sang it with our arms stretched high. We sang it with our heads thrown back and at the top of our lungs. The worship went on and on until we lost all sense of time and our fingertips seemed to touch the edge of heaven. Just when I thought the volume would blow the stadium roof off, the arena erupted in thunderous applause to God.

I thought that beautiful roar sounded a lot like heaven.

Never had I reached so deep into my soul to worship the Lord. Yet the deeper my expression of worship became, the more desperate I felt to do something more. At one point I turned and shouted to a friend, "I want to worship more deeply,

We will desperately long to do something more.

but I can't find any place to go!"

Years later, the sound of those men's voices united in praise still echoes in my memory. I remember, too, what I felt in my own heart that day. And I can imagine when I'm worshiping in the very presence of God with an innumerable host, I'll feel it a hundred times more. That's why I think in heaven I'll feel something close to...*desperation.*

Does that word surprise you?

When you and I stand together in the presence of God—knowing and seeing who He is and all that He has done in His sovereign power to move us from birth to "that Day"—we will pour out our thanks and praise to Him, joyfully doing our best to shake the rafters of heaven.

But I'm also convinced that we will desperately long to do something more.

That's what this chapter is about.

What You Will Crave

The words and example of Jesus, along with my experience in the Silverdome, convince me that *in heaven we will desperately crave to serve.*

When we see our Savior, we will be swept up in a

consuming, eternity-long desire to respond in love to Jesus—and worship and praise won't be enough. We will want to *do* something for Him.

Think about it: When you and I love someone with all our heart, words are wonderful and precious, but we're compelled to go beyond words to action. We long to give, to help, to protect, to serve.

Words weren't enough for God, either.

Words weren't enough for God, either. He loved every person in His world so much that He did something dramatic: He gave His Son in order to save us (John 3:16). And Jesus said that the greatest expression of love is to do something—"to lay down one's life for his friends" (John 15:13).

In this chapter we'll see the direct connection between how well we manage our life for God on earth and how much our Lord will graciously allow us to serve Him in heaven.

THE QUESTION OF YOUR LIFE

Again and again, Jesus told stories about servants commissioned to take care of a valuable asset that belonged to the master (for example, money, fields, or vineyards). A helpful word to describe this role and one the Bible uses is *steward*.

What distinguishes a steward from a servant? Both a steward and a servant serve someone, both have a responsibility, and both work for a wage. The difference is that a steward has been charged with managing his master's assets. In Jesus' stories, we often see a pattern: The servant/steward is charged with managing something important for his master while the master is away for an extended period.

Picture the key events of a steward's service in a timeline:

Begin .... *End*

The Commission of the Steward	The Master Leaves	The Opportunity of the Steward	The Master Returns	The Reward of the Steward

You can easily identify the one step where the steward has the chance to either fail or succeed at his mission and impact his future—it is his "opportunity."

Jesus told parables about stewards for an important and specific reason: He would soon be going away. During His absence, the business of His kingdom on earth would be delegated to His followers. They would be commissioned to spend their lives greatly increasing His kingdom. In the future He would return, ask for an accounting, and reward His servants "each according to his works" (Matthew 16:27).

If you are a Christian, you are in the same circumstance as the early followers of Jesus.

You have been commissioned to manage an asset for your Master. Your asset is your life—the sum of your talents, strengths, personality, and interests. Your opportunity is to manage your life in such a way that you greatly increase your Master's kingdom. Your Master has not yet returned, and every day you should answer this question:

How will I steward what my Master has placed in my care?

A LIFE GOD REWARDS

> *The stewards' assignment? "Do business till I come."*

In fact, every day you *are* answering this question. In the parables we're about to look at, this truth is quietly but plainly evident. Whether you act intentionally on your commission or not, you are deciding by your actions and attitudes how you will steward your opportunity for God.

Since our Master is not physically present, good stewardship always requires faith—faith that our Master is who He said He is, faith that what He asked us to do matters now and will matter when He returns, and faith that He *will* return.

No wonder the Bible uses the word *faithful* more than any other to describe the conduct of a good steward. Paul said that the one nearly defined the other: "It is required in stewards that one be found faithful" (1 Corinthians 4:2).

"Do Business Till I Come"

Jesus' two best-known parables about stewardship, the Parable of the Minas and the Parable of the Talents, both start with ordinary people in ordinary situations but quickly enter into surprising territory.

In the Parable of the Minas, found in Luke 19, a nobleman must leave town. He calls ten servants and gives each one a mina (about three years' wages). The stewards' assignment? "Do business till I come" (v. 13).

When the nobleman returns, he calls for an accounting. The first servant reports a tenfold increase on his investment of his master's mina. The master responds, "Well done, good servant; because you were faithful in a very little, have authority over ten cities" (v. 17).

The second servant reports a fivefold return, and the master gives him an exactly proportionate reward: "You also be over five cities" (v. 19). Yet what is most notable is what the master *doesn't* say to him—he doesn't say, "Well done," or "good servant," or even "because you were faithful in a very little." The lesser level of commendation shows that the Master knew the servant could have done more to multiply his mina.

The third steward simply returns the mina he was given, explaining that he kept the money safely hidden at home.

Imagine his shame when his master calls him a "wicked servant" (v. 22), then takes his one mina and gives it to the servant who already had ten! The nobleman explains his action with a startling statement: "To everyone who has will be given; and from him who does not have, even what he has will be taken away from him" (v. 26).

Does the nobleman's response seem fair to you?

When I teach on this parable, audiences often rush to defend the third servant. "Wasn't he just being careful?" they say. "Besides, he didn't *lose* anything." Yet it doesn't take long, as we talk about how we make decisions as parents, managers, or owners, for us to agree: We invariably give the greatest future opportunity to the person who has proven to be the most productive with the present opportunity.

Audiences often rush to defend the third servant.

Fortunately for us, Jesus' parable shows the responses of all three stewards—and we can discover life-changing insights from each.

Great Expectations

Let's look at three common misbeliefs about stewardship among Christians today and the corresponding truth Jesus wants us to see:

- We think that even though God gave us our gifts and talents, He is not bothered if we don't make the most of every opportunity.

But the *Truth of the First Steward* shows us that God expects us to take the resources of our lives and *greatly multiply* them for His kingdom.

- We think that if God does reward us for serving Him, His reward will be a general commendation that will apply to everyone equally and won't change our future opportunities in His kingdom.

But the *Truth of the Second Steward* is that God will reward our work for Him, but it will be in direct *proportion* to how much we have multiplied our life for Him. His response will have a major and eternal impact on our future.

- We think that if we don't serve God with what He's given us, the worst that could happen would be no reward.

But the *Truth of the Third Steward* is that if we do not use what God has placed in our care for Him, we will *suffer loss*—of both the potential reward we could have earned, and the opportunity to serve God more fully in eternity.

TEN-MINA MAN

I remember when the radical implications of these truths exploded into my mind and heart. Although I was very familiar with the parable, I'd never asked myself: *Am I a ten-mina steward?*

The question launched a season of sober reevaluation and radical change in my life. Finally, a breakthrough came. I chose to believe that since a ten-mina life was God's purpose for me, I would take it as the best measure of stewardship in my life. I committed to God that by His grace I would become a ten-mina man for Him.

But maybe by now you're thinking, *I don't have*

many talents or opportunities, so how can I bring God much return for my life? And does that mean I won't have the chance to serve Him much in eternity?

An encouraging answer from Jesus is found in the Parable of the Talents (Matthew 25:14–30). The story follows the same pattern as the Parable of the Minas. But this time, three stewards are each given *different amounts* of money—"to each according to his own ability" (v. 15).

In this case, two servants double what they have been given. Yet when the master returns, he gives the *same commendation and reward* to both. Why? Because a servant's reward is based on total results *in light of potential*. The master tells both servants the same thing:

> *"Well done, good and faithful servant; you were faithful over a few things, I will make you ruler over many things. Enter into the joy of your lord."*
>
> VV. 21, 23

In the same way, Jesus will reward you and me on the basis of what each of us did with what we were given.

Are you a seamstress or the leader of a nation? A factory worker or a young mother? A village pastor or a builder? Every disciple has the same opportunity for productivity now, and the same opportunity for great reward later. In fact, your future is as promising and important as the future of the most gifted person in history.

For Sheila, a mother of toddlers, ten-mina living has meant turning sincere intentions into a sensible plan—a weekly friendship group for struggling young moms in her neighborhood.

For Mark, a developer in Arizona, ten-mina living has meant redefining what "do business" implies. Increasingly, he is rearranging his workload so he can spend the majority of his time providing building services at no cost to mission projects in Central America.

For Jennifer, who went blind at the age of fifteen, ten-mina living has meant that boundary lines have become starting lines. She now calls her blindness "my difficult gift" and is reaching thousands through music and speaking.

I hope you never again think of faithfully serving God as merely not sinning a lot, doing "business as usual," or just not quitting. True faithfulness as a steward is much closer to *extraordinary entrepreneurial excellence!*

THE STEWARD'S REWARD

I opened this chapter telling you why I believed we will desperately want to serve God in heaven. *Doing* is a servant's language of devotion. In heaven, more opportunity to do God's will through loving service will be our highest reward.

Exactly how *much* opportunity will faithful stewards receive in heaven? So much that in the upside-down kingdom of heaven, the highest word for serving is *ruling*. We can trace this surprising reversal to the Garden of Eden. Remember that at Creation God made both woman and man for a particular task—to serve Him on earth by stewarding His creation. Jesus confirmed this purpose when He told His disciples that their reward in heaven for serving Him here would be to sit on twelve thrones and judge the tribes of Israel (Matthew 19:28).

Doing is a servant's language of devotion.

Your commission for Jesus is as big as the world.

Ruling in heaven will have *nothing* in common with the corruption and manipulation we're so used to seeing in displays of power on earth! When the curse of sin is removed and you and I are restored to our creation purpose, we will be free to rule for God to our fullest powers while bringing only the highest good to ourselves and to others.

Ruling is also the reward for serving we see in Jesus' parables of faithful stewards. Did you notice? In the mina parable, the highest reward for service was to "have authority over ten cities" (Luke 19:17). And in the Parable of the Talents, the reward is similar—"I will make you ruler over many things" (Matthew 25:21, 23).

Serve faithfully here, rule perfectly there.

My friend, I challenge you to see your true calling today and to seize the opportunity that is right in front of you. Don't waste another day living for less. Your commission for Jesus is as big as the world

(Mark 16:15). Your opportunity is now. Serve Him faithfully on earth and you will be wonderfully, fully, perfectly prepared to do what you will desperately crave to do in heaven.

And on that Day, you will hear Jesus tell you from His heart, "Well done, good and faithful servant...enter into the joy of your Lord."

6

The God Who Gives Back

"Do not lay up for yourselves treasures on earth, where moth and rust destroy and where thieves break in and steal; but lay up for yourselves treasures in heaven, where neither moth nor rust destroys and where thieves do not break in and steal."

Jesus, in Matthew 6:19–20

I was taking a coffee break during a family conference in Kentucky when Will walked up and stood beside my chair. He was about nine. He asked if I wanted to donate to a missions project.

"What would you use my money for?" I asked.

Will held out a radio. "This radio runs by sun power," he said proudly. "It's for people who live in the jungles. People can listen to this radio to learn things and hear about Jesus."

I decided on the spot to make Will an offer. "Tell

you what," I said, "I'll give to your project, but I have a rule that says you have to give money first." On one of his donation cards, I wrote out my proposal:

Will,
If you give one to five dollars,
    I'll give double what you give.
If you give six to ten dollars,
    I'll give triple what you give.
If you give eleven to twenty dollars,
    I'll give four times what you give.

I signed my name and Will read the card. By the time he was finished, his eyes were as big as saucers. Then suddenly his face fell, and he stared at the floor.

"Don't you like my idea?" I asked.

"Yeah," he said, shuffling his feet.

"Well, what are you going to do?"

"Nothing."

"Nothing?"

"I can't," he said. "I already gave everything I had."

I felt a pang in my heart. "You mean you put all your money in your own fund drive?" I asked.

He nodded.

"So you can't buy any more snacks for the rest of the conference?"

He nodded again.

At that moment, I knew what I needed to do. "Actually, Will," I began, "I also have a rule that if you give everything you have, I will give everything I have, too."

As it happened, I'd just been to a bank to withdraw a considerable amount of cash for my trip. I reached under the table for my briefcase, pulled out a bank envelope of bills, and handed it to Will.

I'm not sure who was more surprised—Will or me. Now both of us had eyes as big as saucers, but we were both grinning happily.

My experience with Will has come to illustrate a truth for me about giving that's so surprising it hardly sounds possible: *Whatever I give to God on earth He will more than give back to me in heaven.*

In this chapter we will explore what Jesus said about how to make our money and possessions count in eternity.

A Generous Matching Plan

What did Jesus really teach about money and possessions?

Peter may have first heard it clearly when he listened to Jesus telling a wealthy young man why he should leave his possessions and money to follow Him: "You will have treasure in heaven" (Matthew 19:21).

When the man turned down Jesus' offer and left, Peter stepped forward to ask the obvious question:

> *"See, we have left all and followed You. Therefore what shall we have?"*
>
> v. 27

I love the fact that Jesus didn't scold Peter for his self-interest. Or smile and say, "I wasn't actually *serious* about treasure in heaven." Instead, He gave a most revealing answer. Jesus told Peter that he and the other disciples would rule over the nation of Israel when He set up His kingdom. Then He said that every person who leaves all to follow Him would be repaid a hundredfold (Matthew 19:29).

A hundredfold is the equivalent of a 10,000 percent return!

Now you can see that what happened to nine-year-old Will only hints at God's amazing plan to reward every believer who sacrifices treasure on earth to serve Him. Suddenly my "generous" matching of Will's donation appears meager next to God's extravagant promise.

What Jesus Said You Should Do with Treasure

Perhaps Jesus' most familiar teaching on treasure is found in the Sermon on the Mount:

> *"Do not lay up for yourselves treasures on earth, where moth and rust destroy and where thieves break in and steal; but lay up for yourselves treasures in heaven."*
>
> Matthew 6:19–20

If you grew up in church like I did, you may assume that these verses mean spiritual pursuits are more important than earthly ones. But Jesus was clearly talking about actual treasure and how you can keep it. He used the same word to describe real treasure on earth and real treasure in heaven (translated *thesauros* in Greek). He didn't reveal what treasure in heaven would look like or how it would be measured, but it *will* be highly valuable.

Jesus shatters three common misconceptions about how we should think about treasure.

Suppose your accountant said to you: "If you invest your treasure in Bank A, you will lose it. But if you invest your treasure in Bank B, you will save it."

You'd never assume that while your accountant referred to your hard-earned money when she mentioned Bank A, she meant only your spiritual treasures when she recommended Bank B! Why, then, should we think that eternal treasure will be anything less than real and highly desirable?

Here, in just one verse (Matthew 6:20), Jesus shatters three common misconceptions about how we should think about treasure:

1. *What you should do with your treasure—"lay up."* The Greek verb, translated "lay up," is in the imperative in this verse—it's Jesus' command. He wants you to know that laying up treasure is God's plan for you and is a directive you should obey.
2. *Who you should lay it up for—"yourselves."* Each of us must lay up treasure individually. Jesus reveals that if you don't lay up treasure for yourself in heaven, no one can do it for you. That's why Jesus called the man who never laid up treasure for himself a "fool" (Luke 12:13–21). Jesus never rewards selfishness, only *selflessness*. As you're going to see, to lay up treasure for ourselves in heaven, we must first give it to others on earth.
3. *Where you should lay it up—"in heaven."* Location matters. If you lay up treasure on earth, as Jesus pointed out, it's vulnerable to corruption or loss. The truth is that heaven is the only place where your treasure will be safe.

By now you might be asking, "But why would treasure matter to me in heaven?"

I understand the question. Yet we have to conclude from Jesus' dramatic statements here and elsewhere that our treasure will matter greatly to us in eternity!

In God's kingdom, when the sinful pull of greed, envy, and manipulation is absent, we will *enjoy* our treasure, and it will serve a pure and meaningful purpose. As we'll see, our treasure will allow us to serve, to give, to accomplish, and to enjoy more for Him.

But there's something very specific we must do, Jesus said, to "transfer" our treasure to heaven.

Getting It from Here to There

I remember years ago, when Darlene Marie and I moved across the country. As we stood in our driveway watching the moving truck pull away, it occurred to me that aside from the bare essentials, the truck contained our most important belongings and personal treasures. Since our plan was to follow later by car, we wouldn't see our possessions again until weeks later, when we arrived at our new home.

We forward the treasure of our lives on to heaven a lot like that. We stay behind with the essentials. But the real goods—if we intend to keep their value through eternity—must go on ahead.

Think of it as God's moving plan: *To move your treasure to heaven, you have to send it ahead.*

How do we accomplish that? One day, Jesus explained His moving plan to His disciples:

> *"Sell what you have and give alms; provide yourselves money bags which do not grow old, a treasure in the heavens that does not fail, where no thief approaches nor moth destroys."*
>
> LUKE 12:33

This verse clearly shows the link between an action regarding treasure on earth and the result of that action in heaven. If you "give alms" now, Jesus told His friends, you will actually "provide [for] yourselves" something valuable later—"a treasure in the heavens."

I hope it's evident to you that Jesus wasn't telling His disciples that treasure doesn't matter, or that He didn't want them to have any. Just the opposite! He wanted them to provide for themselves *because* He knew that treasure will matter in eternity, and He wanted them to have a lot of it there.

Paul told Timothy to command the well-to-do members of his church to "be rich in good works, ready to give, willing to share, *storing up for themselves a good foundation for the time to come*" (1 Timothy 6:18–19).

Notice the pattern of teaching: Followers of Jesus are to store up "for themselves," and the reason lies in the unbreakable link—their action affects "the time to come."

Do you want to store up "treasure in the heavens that does not fail"? Then surrender it to God's priorities here. That is the only way.

Everything You Own Is on Loan

Just as you'd expect, the principles of stewardship (responsibility, faithfulness, growth, and potential) apply to our treasure.

In one of His teachings about money and possessions in heaven, Jesus said:

> *"He who is faithful in what is least is faithful also in much.... Therefore if you have not been faithful in the unrighteous mammon, who will commit to your trust the true riches? And if you have not been faithful in what is another man's, who will give you what is your own?"*
>
> Luke 16:10–12

Here, Jesus is describing how a steward can succeed with someone else's money. Not surprisingly, He uses the word *faithful* four times!

What *is* surprising is what Jesus promises a faithful steward of treasure. It is not, as you might expect, that you will steward more treasure in heaven, but that you will *own* it. Instead of having the "unrighteous mammon" of earth, you will have the "true riches" of heaven; instead of managing "what is another man's," you will have "what is your own."

In other words, if you do well with what you *think* is your own now, you'll get what is *really* your own later.

The Sum of Your Opportunities

You can probably look around your circle of acquaintances and find your own favorite examples of giving away earthly treasure. Here are a few of mine:

- Marcellus gave away his entire wardrobe to homeless men (and Marcellus is a man of exceptional taste in clothing).
- Ira and Francis cashed in a retirement fund so they could support themselves while they volunteered full-time at a drug treatment program.

- Seven men shaved off all their hair to show support for a dying friend who had lost his hair because of cancer treatments.
- Mariba gave her most cherished painting to a discouraged friend.
- Nathan and Anna sold their large home and downsized so they could free up substantial funds for God's work.

No matter how large or small your gift, you put your life in motion by answering two simple questions:

1. *"What treasure has God given me?"* The same principle of potential we saw in the last chapter also applies to stewarding treasure. God evaluates faithfulness based on our potential—how much we give of what He has entrusted us with. Jesus commended the widow for giving her pennies because proportionately she was giving far more than the rich (Luke 21:4).
2. *"What is God asking me to do with my treasure?"* After giving to the church, ask God for guidance about where to give beyond that. One investment is not as good as another. Ask yourself what God cares

about most. For example, will directing your giving to a high-profile civic fund please Him as much as giving it to your church's missions fund?

The solution is simple, probably difficult, and absolutely life changing.

The people I've met who are most faithful with their money are also the most free of its entanglements. They are the ones I admire most, because they understand that if you don't serve God with your money, you will serve your money.

A RIVAL MASTER

The treasure God asks you to serve Him with is the very force in your life that threatens your loyalties to your Master. Jesus said:

> *"No servant can serve two masters; for either he will hate the one and love the other, or else he will be loyal to the one and despise the other. You cannot serve God and mammon."*
>
> LUKE 16:13

When you serve God, you are using God's money to accomplish His wishes. But when you serve money, you are using God's money to accomplish your wishes. And when you do that, you will inevitably follow your human instincts to keep your money *here*.

But Jesus said, "Where your treasure is, there your heart will be also" (Matthew 6:21).

So let me ask you, where is your heart right now? If you aren't purposefully and generously investing your treasure in God's kingdom, I promise you it's because your heart isn't there.

The solution is simple, probably difficult, and absolutely life changing. Don't wait for your heart to move on its own, my friend, because it might never happen. Instead, apply what you've learned from the words of Jesus. Begin to move your treasure today to what matters in heaven…and your heart will follow.

7

THE FIRST KEY

"For God did not send His Son into the world to condemn the world, but that the world through Him might be saved."

JESUS, IN JOHN 3:17

Rudy had that look. His wife had just introduced him to me at the front of the church, then "unexpectedly" left to attend to other matters. Rudy stood there awkwardly, hands shoved in his pockets. I'm sure he would have given half his life savings to be delivered from my presence.

I smiled and asked how I could help.

"My wife wants me to get religion," he said, scuffing the carpet with the toe of his shoe.

I asked him why.

He grimaced. "So I don't go to hell."

"Are you planning to go to hell sometime soon?" I asked.

He looked at me, then burst out laughing. He seemed relieved to find that a Bible teacher might have a sense of humor.

"So," I continued, "when you stand before God, what's going to keep you out of hell?"

Dead silence, then Rudy chuckled. "I guess I never thought about it quite like that." He continued hesitantly, "I'm not a bad person, you know. I don't run around on my wife like some of my friends. And I try to be a nice guy most of the time...."

I decided to help him out. "So God probably has a big scale, wouldn't you think? On one side would be your sins—you do sin, don't you, Rudy?"

He nodded.

I continued. "And on the other would be all those

A smile crossed his face. He liked how my answer was shaping up.

good things you do for your wife, your kids, your community, and so on. Am I on the right track?"

Rudy nodded with more enthusiasm.

"And when God puts your life on His big scale, you'll have more good than bad, and everything will be okay, right?"

A smile crossed his face. He liked how my answer was shaping up. I told him that it all made sense to me, too, but I had a question. I took out my pen and drew a line like this:

TOTALLY EVIL ———————————— TOTALLY GOOD
(0 percent good)   *(100 percent good)*

"Clearly," I said, "you just need to decide how much more good than bad you need for the scale to tilt in your favor." I handed Rudy my pen and asked him to put an *x* on the line to mark how close to "Totally Good" he'd have to get to be good enough for heaven.

Rudy studied my pad, then started to mark an *x* at about 60 percent. Then he reconsidered and moved it closer to 75 percent, then paused to think again. Finally he shook his head and drew a rather feeble *x* at about the 70 percent spot.

He handed me back my pen without looking up.

I pointed to his mark. "Let's say you hit your spot right on the nose, Rudy, because you really aren't that bad of a guy. But what if when you meet your Maker He reveals to you that, unfortunately, the x spot is farther to the right—say at 71 percent. If you were 70 percent 'good' but God said the minimum required was actually 71 percent, where would a person like you go?"

He crossed his arms, still not looking at me. "Hell, I guess."

"Then finding out where the actual x is on that line would be the most important question of your life, right?" I asked.

That was the day my new friend hit God's mark perfectly.

Rudy grunted in agreement.
"Yeah, I'm just not too sure where it ought to be."

I closed my notepad and started picking up my things, but Rudy wasn't moving. "Can I know exactly where the x is?" he asked. "Cause I really need to know. Maybe you could take another minute and show me?"

I was hoping he would feel that way. We found a seat in a quiet corner, and I showed him what the Bible says about that *x*. He understood, he responded…and that was the day my new friend hit God's mark perfectly.

THE NAME OF THE PROBLEM

The first six chapters of the book focused on the second key to your eternity—how your works affect your repayment in heaven. It's time to talk about the first key. As you may recall, the first key is *belief*—what you believe determines where you will spend your forever.

In a book where there has been so much talk about what you need to *do* to get the most out of your life, you're going to love what you learn about the key of belief. The teachings of Jesus show us that our belief works where our works don't—and for a very important reason.

Someone has already done the work for you!

Someone or something had put it in Rudy's mind that if he wanted to gain entrance to heaven, he had a problem that only good works could fix. Millions of thoughtful people around the world think the same

The First Key

way. But according to Jesus, Rudy and all those millions of others are trying to solve the right problem with the wrong key.

Let me show you what I mean.

Notice that it never entered Rudy's mind that his standing with God was secure—because he knew it wasn't. He had a problem, and it's that very problem that he was trying to fix with his good works. The name for this problem is sin. Everyone knows by experience that they have sinned repeatedly.

Paul wrote that it is God who plants this awareness in us:

> *For the wrath of God is revealed from heaven against all ungodliness and unrighteousness of men, who suppress the truth in unrighteousness, because what may be known of God is manifest in them, for God has shown it to them.*
>
> ROMANS 1:18–19

And because God also reveals His existence and His attributes to us, said Paul, this awareness of our sin problem leaves us without excuse:

> *For since the creation of the world His invisible attributes are clearly seen, being understood by the things that are made, even His eternal power and Godhead, so that they are without excuse, because, although they knew God, they did not glorify Him as God.*
>
> VV. 20–21

These verses sum up the very real human problem that every major religion in the world is trying to solve: *Since we know that we deserve God's judgment, what can we do to make things right with Him and escape the consequences of our sin?*

Some religions seek to appease the spirit world through activities such as animal sacrifices or paying money to a witch doctor or shaman. Some religions teach that people can atone for sin by enduring suffering now—for example, crawling for miles on their knees, or beating themselves—so they won't suffer later. Other religions teach that people can make up for their wrongs by doing more right. That was Rudy's religion.

But none of these religious approaches can solve the universal problem of sin. Why? Because they rely on our good works, and as we'll see in a minute, the consequences of our sin are so severe that no amount of good works on our part can rescue us.

Jesus taught that your works for God on earth can greatly benefit you in eternity once your sin problem has been resolved and heaven is your destination. But this raises a sobering question: What value, if any, could good works have in eternity if you haven't yet resolved your sin problem and hell is your destination?

No amount of good works on our part can rescue us.

Jesus showed that although good works are useless to get anyone into heaven, *they still matter.*

Hell by Degrees

Has it ever bothered you to think that your scrupulously moral and kind neighbor who does not believe in Jesus will suffer to the same degree as Hitler in eternity? Something deep in your spirit says that wouldn't be fair.

That's because it wouldn't be.

If the unbreakable link—which says that actions on earth have consequences in eternity—applies equally to every person, it should apply whether your destination is heaven or hell.

In fact, since Jesus reveals that there will be degrees of reward in heaven, wouldn't it make sense that a just God would judge nonbelievers in the same way—with degrees of retribution?

> *It's time to tell you what I told Rudy.*

That's exactly what Jesus said. Specifically, He revealed that suffering in hell has the potential to increase according to how a person lived his life. We see this truth first in Jesus' condemnation:

> *"And you, Capernaum…will be brought down to Hades; for if the mighty works which were done in you had been done in Sodom, it would have remained until this day. But I say to you that it shall be more tolerable for the land of Sodom in the day of judgment than for you."*
>
> MATTHEW 11:23–24

The First Key

Notice the phrase *more tolerable*. The word *more* in that phrase indicates that different degrees of tolerability and judgment exist in hell.

On another occasion, Jesus told the Pharisees that they would "receive greater condemnation" for using their position to prey on widows and for making long prayers for pretense (Matthew 23:14). The apostle Paul wrote that some were "treasuring up for [themselves] wrath in the day of wrath" (Romans 2:5). The apostle John said that unbelievers would be judged, "each one according to [in proportion to] his works" (Revelation 20:13).

But don't be confused: Your good works can never lessen the torment of hell, in the same way that an evil work (sin) can't lessen the joys of heaven. Here's a helpful way to remember the truth of degrees of compensation:

Heaven never gets worse, only better;
hell never gets better, only worse.

Isn't it time for you to pick up on the only key that will unlock heaven for you? Now it's time to tell you what I told Rudy.

Why Works Won't Work

Rudy was ready to learn where the x should go. I pointed to the "100 percent good" mark and said, "The Bible says that's where the x has to be."

"But that's impossible!" Rudy replied. "Then no one would go to heaven."

"So you agree that no one can be 100 percent good and solve the problem of sin on his own?"

"Yes, I guess so."

"And what if I told you that the penalty for sin—for even one sin—is death?"

"Well, that wouldn't seem fair at all," he said. "No one's perfect. Everyone sins—but the punishment is still death?"

I reassured Rudy that he was thinking logically. Then I opened my Bible and showed him that ever since Adam and Eve sinned in the Garden, death—both physical and spiritual—has been the consequence. In Genesis we read, "For in the day that you eat of it you shall surely die" (Genesis 2:17). And in the New Testament, Rudy saw that the problem is still with us: "For the wages of sin is *death*" (Romans 6:23).

"Think of it this way," I continued. "Let's say I went before a judge and was sentenced to die. But I told the judge, 'Please, sir, let me live, and I promise I'll do a lot of community service.' Would that work?"

"Of course not!" said Rudy. After a minute he said, "So there's no solution, is there? There's no hope."

"Exactly," I said. "There's no hope—" I paused for a moment before continuing—"unless you could find a substitute. What if someone volunteered to substitute for you—to stand in your place—when it came time for God to judge you?"

"That would be great," he said. "But you said they'd have to be 100 percent good, and no one is, right?"

"Exactly—no one except Jesus." I went on to explain to Rudy that the Bible says Jesus was God's Son and He alone lived on this earth without sin. In fact, God sent His Son to earth so that He could be Rudy's substitute, die in Rudy's place, and pay the penalty for his sin—and the whole world's sin—once and for all.

Then I pulled out my notebook again. I pointed to

the *x* Rudy had drawn. "You have a choice to make, Rudy."

"Okay," he said.

I pointed at his *x*. "You can believe in your good works—and hope you're right about the *x*. Or you can believe in Jesus Christ and His death on your behalf."

I urge you to believe that what Jesus said is true.

"Definitely the second choice," he said. "It makes way more sense."

I opened my Bible and read to Rudy how Jesus explained the choice that lay before him.

> *"For God so loved the world that He gave His only begotten Son, that whoever believes in Him should not perish but have everlasting life. For God did not send His Son into the world to condemn the world, but that the world through Him might be saved."*
>
> JOHN 3:16–17

Friend, maybe it's the choice before you, too.

If you have been reading this chapter and you're

not sure that heaven is your destination, I urge you to put your faith in what Jesus said. If you want to put your full trust in Him, then why not pray the same prayer Rudy did:

Dear God, I am sorry for my sins, and now I know I can't do anything to fix them. So I accept Your Son's death as full payment for my sins, and I receive the Lord Jesus Christ as my Savior. And Jesus, I'm going to start serving You right now! In Your name, amen.

This is a prayer God always answers and is delighted to hear.

DESTINATION HEAVEN

If you just put your full trust in Jesus for your salvation, your eternal destination has already permanently changed—from hell to heaven!

Now you are a new creation in Jesus (2 Corinthians 5:17). Now you have eternal life (John 3:16–17). Now you are a child of God and an heir of salvation (Galatians 4:7).

And from this moment on, you don't have to hope that your good works will add up to your salvation, because like every other true follower of Jesus, you now understand the meaning of these well-known verses:

> *By grace you have been saved through faith, and that not of yourselves; it is the gift of God, not of works, lest anyone should boast.*
>
> EPHESIANS 2:8–9

Because of this grace, you will never experience in eternity the negative consequences of your sins—because Jesus took those on Himself.

Instead, you can begin responding with your whole heart of love for God and with service for Him, knowing that He will want to reward you for everything you do for Him.

Look at the very next verse:

> *For we are His workmanship, created in Christ Jesus for good works, which God prepared beforehand that we should walk in them.*
>
> V. 10

You, my friend, have been created and saved to do good works!

And if you just placed your trust in Jesus Christ, then for the first time in your life, you are truly ready to live a life God rewards.

8

SEEING THROUGH TO FOREVER

"And behold, I am coming quickly, and My reward is with Me, to give to every one according to his work."

JESUS, IN REVELATION 22:12

When your alarm clock goes off tomorrow morning, eternity will be nowhere in sight.

You'll put on your eyeglasses, fumble with your collar. You'll greet your family, have a strong cup of coffee or tea, walk out into your day...and make the first choice of your new life.

Will I live for what I can see, knowing it will soon disappear? Or will I live for eternity?

This book has tried to show you beyond all doubt

what Jesus wanted you to know so you could make the right choice.

Yet no matter how hard you look, you won't find visible proof of your future in heaven. Why? "We do not look at the things which are seen," wrote Paul, "but at the things which are not seen. For the things which are seen are temporary" (2 Corinthians 4:18).

Earth may be temporary, but it sure is convincing, isn't it? Without faith, we could never see or even imagine our true destination.

I'll never forget hearing the story in graduate school of a missionary couple from Great Britain who had spent a lifetime serving God in some far corner of the earth. The century turned. After forty years, they wrote their supporters that they were coming home and sailed for England.

When they laid eyes on their country's coastline for the first time in decades, the man said to his wife, "I wonder if anyone will be here to welcome us home."

As the ship sailed into Plymouth Harbor, the elderly couple stood at the upper deck of the ocean liner, holding hands. Then, to their surprise and pleasure, they saw that throngs of people crowded the

Earth may be temporary, but it sure is convincing, isn't it?

dock, pointing in their direction and cheering. A band played. Men held up a banner that read, "Welcome home! We're proud of you!"

The husband was deeply moved. "Isn't this wonderful!" His wife laughed happily, and they decided it was time to go below to collect their luggage.

But as they emerged onto the gangplank, their hearts pounding with anticipation, they were taken aback. The crowd had already started to disperse. Soon, it became clear what had happened. The huge welcome was not for them, but for a politician returning from some foreign success. In fact, no one was there to greet them at all.

The husband couldn't hide his disappointment. "After a lifetime of service, this isn't much of a welcome home."

His wife took his arm. "Come along, sweetheart," she said softly. "This is just England. We're not home yet."

THE BOOK OF REMEMBRANCE

Doesn't it strike you that a major reason so many followers of Jesus are not wholeheartedly serving God is that we base our expectation of reward on visible proof? We may not often admit it, but we expect an immediate consequence for our good choices; then if we don't see one, *we conclude that there must be no eternal consequence.*

I remember several hundred Christian workers at a retreat in the Midwest who had been temporarily blinded by the immediate. By our second day together, the depth of their discouragement became obvious. I asked, "How many of you would say that even though you love God, right now you feel ready to give up? For what you put into your ministry, it just isn't worth it?"

More than half raised a hand.

Together we opened our Bibles to the last page of the Old Testament. There we met another group of God's servants who wanted to live for God but were seeing no benefit. In fact, they had concluded based on what they could see that those who didn't give God's will a second thought seemed more blessed than they (Malachi 3:15). Here is what they said:

"It is useless to serve God;
What profit is it that we have kept His ordinance?"

v. 14

Do you wonder how God would respond to such an honest and painful complaint? What follows is one of the Bible's most tender moments. God listens. He understands that they are men and women caught in time, easily losing perspective, losing hope that God is even paying attention. The Bible records:

And the LORD listened and heard them;
So a book of remembrance was written
before Him
For those who fear the LORD
And who meditate on His name.

v. 16

Why is God writing a book of remembrance? To reassure His people that He does watch and care. And at a point in the future, He will reveal its contents. Read on:

"On the day that I make them My jewels....
You shall again discern...

Between one who serves God
And one who does not serve Him."

VV. 17–18

What a picture of God's love and fairness! Whatever things might look like right now, on a day in the future, He will open His book of remembrance, and the truth about His generosity, faithfulness, and justice will be evident to all. Not one act of service in His name will have gone unnoticed or unrewarded.

As the roomful of believers at that retreat saw the truth, their discouragement fled. Some shed tears as they realized how much they'd underestimated their King. Many gladly recommitted themselves to His service. How could they not, they said, when He'd promised to one day make everything wonderfully right?

Before we closed that session, I showed them something else amazing in the Bible about that Day. Now I want to show you.

THE JESUS OF THE LAST PAGE

If you're a parent, you probably know that feeling of looking into your child's upturned face and realizing

> *Not one act of service in His name will have gone unnoticed.*

that you hold it in your power to make her biggest wish come true, *and then some!*

That's how Jesus feels about you right now.

You see, the message at the close of the Old Testament is repeated at the close of the New. If you turn to the last page of Revelation, you can read it. You'll find it in the final promise of Jesus:

> *"Behold, I am coming quickly, and My reward is with Me, to give to every one according to his work."*
>
> REVELATION 22:12

I'm struck by the fact that Jesus doesn't say, "I'm coming quickly to set up My kingdom." You see, He cares most about the *people* of His kingdom—people who have given a lifetime to Him because they believed what He said, and they wanted to please Him, and they chose to be faithful.

Do you see your God in a fresh light? He is a God who notices and cares about your every attempt, no matter how small, to serve Him. He sees your upturned face, knows your heart, and cares about your faithfulness.

He promises to reward you...and He can't wait to do so!

Living toward Your "Well Done!"

I remember when Darlene Marie and I first chose to believe in God's eternal reward and to live for that Day. It dramatically changed our actions and priorities. It reordered how our family handled our money, our time, and our abilities. It added new, obvious urgency to how we tended to unfinished business. We became more grateful, more overwhelmed by the kindness of God.

And we began to live every day for the Rewarder's "Well done."

Since then, we've met hundreds of other men and women who, at Jesus' invitation, have looked into eternity and are now on an outrageous mission—to live for God's pleasure.

We became more grateful, more overwhelmed by the kindness of God.

They are wealthy businessmen who have told us they "owned" nothing, not even their shoes. They are students who see an adventure for God in every new face, every difficult class and belittling job. They are young mothers who enthusiastically serve a great King, realizing that their most important work for all of eternity might be the little ones sleeping in the nursery or toddling down the hall.

These exuberant pilgrims seem a lot like other people on the surface, but they understand a day's possibilities from a completely different point of view. Every day is a new opportunity to discover what eternal business might be lurking in the ordinary business of being human.

Sure, they are living *in* the dot, but they are living *for* the line. They're making a difference for God on the streets of New Delhi and Manchester and Lagos and Biloxi....

But they are already citizens of heaven.

Change of Address

Friend, I believe that God is asking you to make a life-changing decision before you leave this book. You need to change your citizenship from earth to heaven.

When Jesus was preparing to leave His disciples, He talked about that place. Listen to His words:

> *"In My Father's house are many mansions; if it were not so, I would have told you. I go to prepare a place for you. And if I go and prepare a place for you, I will come again and receive you to Myself; that where I am, there you may be also."*
>
> JOHN 14:2–3

Think of all the ways Jesus could have described heaven. He could have talked about the streets of gold, the legions of angels, the thrones on which the apostles will sit.

But Jesus wanted His followers to know that heaven was first and foremost...*home*.

The apostle Paul, though he was proud to be both a Jew and a Roman citizen, purposefully chose to think of himself as a citizen of heaven, not of earth

(Philippians 3:20). It was a deep longing to be in heaven with his Lord that occupied his thoughts, shaped his values, and ordered the use of his time. The consequence of Paul's choice continues to impact the world for God today.

If you have heard and understood what Jesus revealed about a life God rewards, and if you're ready to make today count for eternity, I encourage you to join me in declaring your new citizenship:

> *Lord Jesus, I have listened carefully to what You said about my home. I believe You, and I can't wait to be there with You. I renounce my allegiance to this visible and fleeting world and pledge my allegiance to You, King of heaven. From this day on, I will live as a citizen of heaven, my true home. As Your faithful steward, I will take every gift, opportunity, and resource that You place in my hands and multiply it greatly for You. And I eagerly look forward to the day in eternity when I will stand in Your presence, and receive Your reward, and worship You forever.*

Homecoming

Picture your homecoming, the moment when all of eternity and all the angels and saints pause for you. Heaven will hush as you stand before your Savior to hear Him say, "Well done, good and faithful servant!" And then heaven will erupt with welcome and celebration as you accept the incorruptible crown that Jesus is reserving for you.

Heaven will erupt with welcome and celebration.

It will be your unique moment to bless the heart of God. On that day, you will prove that you valued Jesus' death for you, and you gave Him your heart and life in return.

God wants that day, when unseen and eternal things become visible, to be the most wonderful day of your life.

This book is a gift to you for that day, with great anticipation.

Christian Leaders
on Eternal Rewards

Justin Martyr—*Even if we persuade only a few, we shall obtain very great rewards, for, like good laborers, we shall receive recompense from the Master.*

Martin Luther—*Now when Christ says: make to yourselves friends, lay up for yourselves treasures, and the like, you see that he means: do good, and it will follow of itself without your seeking, that you will have friends, find treasures in heaven, and receive a reward.*

John Wesley—*God will reward every one according to his works. But this is well consistent with his distributing advantages and opportunities of improvement, according to his own good pleasure.*

Augustine—*Therefore, we should seek from none other than the Lord God whatever it is that we hope to do well, or hope to obtain as reward for our good works.*

R. C. Sproul—*There are degrees of reward that are given in heaven. I'm surprised that this answer surprises so many people. I think there's a reason Christians are shocked when I say there are various levels of heaven as well as graduations of severity of punishment in hell.*

John Calvin—*Nothing is clearer than that a reward is promised to good works, in order to support the weakness of our flesh by some comfort; but not to inflate our minds with vain glory.*

THEODORE H. EPP—*The primary purpose of the Judgment Seat of Christ is the examination of the lives and service of believers, and the rewarding of them for what God considers worthy of recognition.*

CHARLES R. SWINDOLL—*One of the great doctrines of Christianity is our firm belief in a heavenly home. Ultimately, we shall spend eternity with God in the place He has prepared for us. And part of that exciting anticipation is His promise to reward His servants for a job well done. I don't know many believers in Jesus Christ who never think of being with their Lord in heaven, receiving His smile of acceptance, and hearing His "Well done, good and faithful servant." We even refer to one who died in this way: "He has gone home to his reward."*

JONATHAN EDWARDS—*There are many mansions in God's house because heaven is intended for various degrees of honor and blessedness. Some are designed to sit in higher places there than others; some are designed to be advanced to higher degrees of honor and glory than others are; and, therefore, there are various mansions, and some more honorable mansions and seats, in heaven than others. Though they are all seats of exceeding honor and blessedness yet some more so than others.*

CHARLES H. SPURGEON—*Seek secrecy for your good deeds. Do not even see your own virtue. Hide from yourself that which you yourself have done that is commendable; for the proud contemplation of your own generosity may tarnish all your alms. Keep the thing so secret that even you yourself are hardly aware that you are doing anything at all praiseworthy. Let God be present, and you will have enough of an audience. He will reward you, reward you "openly," reward you as a Father rewards a child, reward you as one who saw what you did, and knew that you did it wholly unto him.*

JOHN MACARTHUR JR.—*There will be varying degrees of reward in heaven. That shouldn't surprise us: There are varying degrees of giftedness even here on earth.*

ORIGEN—*But if it was recorded that my Jesus was received up into glory, I perceive the divine arrangement in such an act, viz., because God, who brought this to pass, commends in this way the Teacher to those who witnessed it, in order that as men who are contending not for human doctrine, but for divine teaching, they may devote themselves as far as possible to the God who is over all, and may do all things in order to please Him, as those who are to receive in the divine judgment the reward of the good or evil which they have wrought in this life.*

CHARLES R. SWINDOLL—*He is waiting to welcome us. To those who serve, to those who stand where Jesus Christ once stood many, many years ago, He promises a reward. And we can be sure He will keep His promise.*

JOHN WESLEY—*Of those who had happily finished their course, such multitudes are afterwards described, and still higher degrees of glory which they attain after a sharp fight and magnificent victory, Rev. 14:1; 15:2; 19:1; 20:4. There is an inconceivable variety in the degrees of reward in the other world. Let not any slothful one say, "If I get to heaven at all, I will be content!" Such a one may let heaven go altogether. In worldly things, men are ambitious to get as high as they can. Christians have a far more noble ambition. The difference between the very highest and the lowest state in the world is nothing to the smallest difference between the degrees of glory.*

CLEMENT OF ALEXANDRIA—*And you know that, of all truths, this is the truest, that the good and godly shall obtain the good reward inasmuch as they held goodness in high esteem; while, on the other hand, the wicked shall receive meet punishment.*

DWIGHT L. MOODY—*If we are Christ's, we are here to shine for Him: by and by He will call us home to our reward.*

JOHN CALVIN—*Conversely, when we see the righteous brought into affliction by the ungodly, assailed with injuries, overwhelmed with calumnies, and lacerated by insult and contumely, while, on the contrary, the wicked flourish, prosper, acquire ease and honour, and all these with impunity, we ought forthwith to infer that there will be a future life in which iniquity shall receive its punishment, and righteousness its reward.*

R. C. SPROUL—*Saint Augustine said that it's only by the grace of God that we ever do anything even approximating a good work, and none of our works are good enough to demand that God reward them. The fact that God has decided to grant rewards on the basis of obedience or disobedience is what Augustine called God's crowning his own works within us. If a person has been faithful in many things through many years, then he will be acknowledged by His Master, who will say to him, "Well done, thou good and faithful servant." The one who squeaks in at the last minute has precious little good works for which he can expect reward.*

THEODORE H. EPP—*God is eager to reward us and does everything possible to help us lay up rewards. But if we are slothful and carnal, so that our service counts for nothing, we shall be saved, yet so as by fire. Let us determine by the grace of God not to be empty handed when we stand before the bema, the Judgment Seat of Christ.*

MARTIN LUTHER—*Therefore, he who does good works and guards himself against sin, God will reward.*

C. S. LEWIS—*If there lurks in most modern minds the notion that to desire our own good and earnestly to hope for the enjoyment of it is a bad thing, I submit that this notion has crept in from Kant and the Stoics and is not part of the Christian faith. Indeed, if we consider the unblushing promises of reward and the staggering nature of the rewards promised in the Gospels, it would seem that Our Lord finds our desires not too strong, but too weak.*

JOHN WESLEY—*For a man cannot profit God. Happy is he who judges himself an unprofitable servant; miserable is he whom God pronounces such. But though we are unprofitable to him, our serving him is not unprofitable to us; for he is pleased to give by his grace a value to our good works which, in consequence of his promise, entitles us to an eternal reward.*

JOHN CALVIN—*Thus Paul enjoins servants, faithfully doing what is of their duty, to hope for recompense from the Lord, but he adds "of the inheritance" (Colossians 3:24).*

R. C. SPROUL—*I'd say there are at least twenty-five occasions where the New Testament clearly teaches that we will be granted rewards according to our works. Jesus frequently holds out the reward motif as the carrot in front of the horse—"great will be your reward in heaven" if you do this or that. We are called to work, to store up treasures for ourselves in heaven, even as the wicked, as Paul tells us in Romans, "treasure up wrath against the day of wrath."*

CHARLES R. SWINDOLL—*On top of these temporal benefits connected to serving, there are eternal rewards as well. Christ Himself, while preparing the Twelve for a lifetime of serving others, promised an eternal reward even for holding out a cup of cool water.*

BILLY GRAHAM—*The believer has his foundation in Jesus Christ. Now we are to build upon this foundation, and the work we have done must stand the ultimate test; final exams come at the Judgment Seat of Christ when we receive our rewards.*

CHARLES STANLEY—*The kingdom of God will not be the same for all believers. Let me put it another way. Some believers will have rewards for their earthly faithfulness; others will not. Some will reign with Christ; others will not (see 2 Tim. 2:12). Some will be rich in the kingdom of God; others will be poor (see Luke 12:21, 33). Some will be given true riches; others will not (see Luke 16:11). Some will be given heavenly treasures of their own; others will not (see Luke 16:12).*

NOTES

CHAPTER 2

Randy Alcorn uses the Dot and Line illustration in his book *The Treasure Principle* (Sisters, Ore.: Multnomah Publishers, 2001).

SOURCES FOR CHRISTIAN LEADERS ON ETERNAL REWARDS

R. C. Sproul quotes excerpted from *Now, That's a Good Question!* by R. C. Sproul © 1996. Used by permission of Tyndale House Publishers, Inc. All rights reserved.

John MacArthur Jr. quote taken from "Bible Questions and Answers," GC 70-13, 1992, cassette. Source: www.biblebb.com/files/macqa/70-13-5.htm. Used by permission.

Theodore H. Epp quotes taken from *Present Labor and Future Rewards* by Theodore H. Epp (Lincoln, Neb.: Back to the Bible, 1960), 78, 86. Used by permission.

C. S. Lewis quote taken from *The Weight of Glory* by C. S. Lewis copyright © C. S. Lewis Pte. Ltd. 1949. Extract reprinted by permission.

Charles Stanley quote reprinted by permission of Thomas Nelson Publishers from the book entitled *Eternal Security* © 1990 by Charles Stanley.

Charles R. Swindoll quotes from *Improving Your Serve* by Charles R. Swindoll © 1981 W Publishing Group, Nashville, Tennessee. All rights reserved.

Billy Graham quote from *Facing Death and the Life After* by Billy Graham © 1987, W Publishing Group, Nashville, Tennessee. All rights reserved.

New companion products for *A Life God Rewards*™

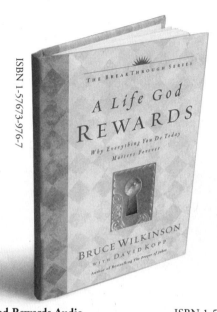

ISBN 1-57673-976-7

- **A Life God Rewards Audio** — ISBN 1-57673-978-3
- **A Life God Rewards Audio CD** — ISBN 1-59052-007-6
- **A Life God Rewards Leather Edition** — ISBN 1-59052-008-4
- **A Life God Rewards Journal** — ISBN 1-59052-010-6
- **A Life God Rewards Devotional** — ISBN 1-59052-009-2
- **A Life God Rewards Bible Study** — ISBN 1-59052-011-4
- **A Life God Rewards Bible Study: Leader's Edition** — ISBN 1-59052-012-2
- **A Life God Rewards Gift Edition** — ISBN 1-59052-949-X

www.thebreakthroughseries.com

God Rewards His Kids

Board Book for Little Ones
ISBN 1-59052-094-7

Specially Illustrated for Kids
ISBN 1-59052-095-5

Begin an Eternal Adventure

Girls Only (Ages 9–12)
ISBN 1-59052-097-1

90-Day Challenge Devotional
ISBN 1-59052-099-8

Guys Only (Ages 9–12)
ISBN 1-59052-096-3

90-Day Challenge Devotional
ISBN 1-59052-098-X

Straight Talk to Teens about Eternity

A Life God Rewards for Teens
ISBN 1-59052-077-7

The BreakThrough Series, Books One and Two

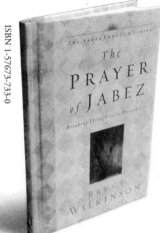

ISBN 1-57673-733-0

"Fastest selling book of all time."
—*Publishers Weekly*

- #1 *New York Times* Bestseller
- Over 9 Million Sold!
- 2001 & 2002 Gold Medallion Book of the Year

ISBN 1-57673-975-9

- *New York Times* Bestseller
- Over 3 Million Sold!

VIDEO, DVD, AUDIO
SERIES

A *Life God Rewards*
BY BRUCE WILKINSON

Audio Cassette Series
US $19.99
Available December 2002

Video Series
US $99.99
Available November 2002
Includes Workbook and Leader's Guide

DVD Series
US $39.99
Available December 2002

Audio CD Series
US $19.99
Available December 2002

Perfect for personal study, small group use, church seminars, church leaders' training, and neighborhood gatherings!

Global Vision
RESOURCES

www.globalvisionresources.com

YOU CAN FIND THESE PRODUCTS AT YOUR LOCAL CHRISTIAN BOOKSTORE.
NOT SURE WHERE THE LOCAL STORE IS?
THIS WEB SITE WILL HELP YOU FIND IT:
http://cba.know-where.com/cba/

The Prayer *of* Jabez

The BreakThrough Series

LITTLE BOOKS | BIG CHANGE

The PRAYER of JABEZ

Breaking Through to the Blessed Life

Dr. Bruce H. WILKINSON

WITH DAVID KOPP

Multnomah® Publishers *Sisters, Oregon*

THE PRAYER OF JABEZ
published by Multnomah Publishers, Inc.

© 2000 by Bruce H. Wilkinson
International Standard Book Numbers:
1-57673-733-0 (Hardback)
1-57673-857-4 (Bonded Leather Edition)

Cover image by Tatsuhiko Shimada/Photonika
Cover design by David Carlson Design

Scipture quotations are from:
The Holy Bible, New King James Version (NKJV)
© 1984 by Thomas Nelson, Inc.

Also quoted: *The Living Bible* (TLB) © 1971. Used by permission of
Tyndale House Publishers, Inc. All rights reserved.

Multnomah is a trademark of Multnomah Publishers, Inc.
and is registered in the U.S. Patent and Trademark Office.
The colophon is a trademark of Multnomah Publishers, Inc.
Printed in the United States of America

ALL RIGHTS RESERVED
No part of this publication may be reproduced, stored in a
retrieval system, or transmitted, in any form or by any means—
electronic, mechanical, photocopying, recording, or otherwise—
without prior written permission.

For information:
MULTNOMAH PUBLISHERS, INC.
POST OFFICE BOX 1720
SISTERS, OREGON 97759

01 02 03 04 05 06 07 08 — 46 45 44 43 42 41 40

Table of Contents

Preface 7

Chapter One — Little Prayer, Giant Prize 9

Chapter Two — So Why Not Ask? 18

Chapter Three — Living Large for God 30

Chapter Four — The Touch of Greatness 45

Chapter Five — Keeping the Legacy Safe 62

Chapter Six — Welcome to God's Honor Roll . . 76

Chapter Seven — Making Jabez Mine 86

*To all who—like those Christians in the
book of Acts—look at who they are now and who
they'll never be, and what they can do now
and what they'll never be able to do…
and still ask God for the world.*

*Without the friendship, commitment and
skill of my writing partner and editor David Kopp,
the early help of my previous editor Larry Libby,
and the encouragement of my publishing friend
John Van Diest, the message of this book would not
have found its way to paper. I am so thankful
that the Lord brought us together.*

Preface

Dear Reader,

I want to teach you how to pray a daring prayer that God always answers. It is brief—only one sentence with four parts—and tucked away in the Bible, but I believe it contains the key to a life of extraordinary favor with God.

This petition has radically changed what I expect from God and what I experience every day by His power. In fact, thousands of believers who are applying its truths are seeing miracles happen on a regular basis.

Will you join me for a personal exploration of Jabez?

I hope you will!

Bruce H. Wilkinson

1

LITTLE PRAYER, GIANT PRIZE

Jabez called on the God of Israel.

The little book you're holding is about what happens when ordinary Christians decide to reach for an extraordinary life—which, as it turns out, is exactly the kind God promises.

My own story starts in a kitchen with yellow counters and Texas-sized raindrops pelting the window. It was my senior year of seminary in Dallas. Darlene, my wife, and I were finding ourselves spending more and more time thinking and praying about what would come next. Where should I throw my energy, passion, and training? What did God want for us as a couple? I stood in our kitchen thinking again about a challenge I'd heard from the seminary chaplain, Dr. Richard Seume. "Want a bigger vision for your life?" he had asked earlier that week. "Sign up to be a gimper for God."

A gimper, as Seume explained it, was someone who always does a little more than what's required or expected. In the furniture business, for example, gimping is putting the finishing touches on the upholstery, patiently applying the ornamental extras that are a mark of quality and value.

Dr. Seume took as his text the briefest of Bible biographies: "Now Jabez was more honorable than his brothers" (1 Chronicles 4:9). Jabez wanted to be more and do more for God, and—as we discover by the end of verse 10—God granted him his request.

End of verse. End of Bible story.

Lord, I think I want to be a gimper for you, I prayed as I looked out the window at the blustery spring rain. But I was puzzled. *What exactly did Jabez do to rise above the rest? Why did God answer his prayer?* I wondered. For that matter, why did God even include Jabez's miniprofile in the Bible?

Maybe it was the raindrops running down the windowpanes. Suddenly my thoughts ran past verse 9.

I picked up my Bible and read verse 10—the prayer of Jabez. Something in his prayer would explain

> *What sentence has revolutionized my life the most?*
> *The cry of a gimper named Jabez.*

the mystery. It had to. Pulling a chair up to the yellow counter, I bent over my Bible, and reading the prayer over and over, I searched with all my heart for the future God had for someone as ordinary as I.

The next morning, I prayed Jabez's prayer word for word.

And the next.

And the next.

Thirty years later, I haven't stopped.

If you were to ask me what sentence—other than my prayer for salvation—has revolutionized my life and ministry the most, I would tell you that it was the cry of a gimper named Jabez, who is still remembered not for what he did, but for what he prayed—and for what happened next.

In the pages of this little book, I want to introduce you to the amazing truths in Jabez's prayer for blessing and prepare you to expect God's astounding answers to it *as a regular part of your life experience.*

How do I know that it will significantly impact you? Because of my experience and the testimony of hundreds of others around the world with whom I've shared these principles. Because, even more importantly, the

Jabez prayer distills God's powerful will for your future. Finally, because it reveals that your Father longs to give you so much more than you may have ever thought to ask for.

Just ask the man who had no future.

THE PRODIGY OF THE GENEALOGY

Someone once said there is really very little difference between people—but that little difference makes a great deal of difference. Jabez doesn't stand astride the Old Testament like a Moses or a David or light up the book of Acts like those early Christians who turned the world upside down. But one thing is sure: The little difference in his life made all the difference.

> *Something about this man caused the historian to pause, clear his throat, and switch tactics.*

You could think of him as the Prodigy of the Genealogy, or maybe the Bible's Little Big Man. You'll find him hiding in the least-read section of one of the least-read books of the Bible.

The first nine chapters of 1 Chronicles are taken up with the official family tree of the Hebrew tribes, beginning with Adam and proceeding through thou-

Little Prayer, Giant Prize

sands of years to Israel's return from captivity. Talk about boring! The long lists of unfamiliar and difficult names—more than five hundred of them—are likely to make even the bravest Bible student turn back.

Take chapter 4. *The descendants of Judah: Perez, Hezron, and Carmi, and Hur, and Shobal....* And that's just the beginning.

Ahumai
Ishma
Idbash
Hazelelponi
Anub...

I'd forgive you if you suddenly considered putting this little book aside and reaching for your TV remote. But stay with me. Because forty-four names into the chapter, a story suddenly breaks through:

> Now Jabez was more honorable than his brothers, and his mother called his name Jabez, saying, "Because I bore him in pain." And Jabez called on the God of Israel saying, "Oh, that You would bless me indeed, and enlarge my territory, that Your hand would be

with me, and that You would keep me from evil, that I may not cause pain!" So God granted him what he requested. (1 Chronicles 4:9–10)

In the next verse, the roll call for the tribe of Judah picks up as if nothing has happened—*Chelub, Shuah, Mehir....*

Something about this man Jabez had caused the historian to pause in middrone, clear his throat, and switch tactics. "Ah, wait a minute!" he seems to interject. "You just *gotta* know something about this guy named Jabez. He stands head and shoulders above the rest!"

Just under the surface of each request lies a giant paradigm breaker.

What was the secret to the enduring reputation of Jabez? You can search from front to back in your Bible, as I have, and you won't find any more information than we have in these two brief verses:

- Things started badly for a person no one had ever heard of.
- He prayed an unusual, one-sentence prayer.

- Things ended extraordinarily well.

Clearly, the outcome can be traced to his prayer. Something about Jabez's simple, direct request to God changed his life and left a permanent mark on the history books of Israel:

> Oh, that You would bless me indeed,
> and enlarge my territory,
> that Your hand would be with me,
> and that You would keep me from evil.

At first glance, the four requests may strike you as sincere, sensible, even noble, but not terribly remarkable. Yet just under the surface of each lies a giant paradigm breaker that runs exactly opposite to the way you and I usually think. In the pages to come, I want to show you just how dramatically each of Jabez's requests can release something miraculous in your life.

LIVING BEYOND THE LIMITS

When was the last time God worked through you in such a way that you knew beyond doubt that God had done it? In fact, when was the last time you saw miracles happen on a regular basis in *your* life? If you're like most believers I've met, you wouldn't know how to ask for that kind of experience, or even if you should.

What I have to share with you has been opening up lives to God's mighty working for many years. Recently, I was in Dallas to teach on the Jabez blessing to an audience of 9,000. Later over lunch, a man said to me, "Bruce, I heard you preach the message of Jabez fifteen years ago, and I haven't stopped praying it. The change has been so overwhelming I have just never stopped."

> *When was the last time God worked through you in such a way that you knew beyond doubt God had done it?*

Across the table, another friend agreed. He said he'd been praying Jabez's little prayer for ten years with similar results. The man next to him, a heart surgeon from Indianapolis, said he had been praying it for five.

I told them, "Friends, I've been praying Jabez for more than *half my life!*"

Because you're reading this book, I believe you share my desire to reach for a life that will be "more honorable" for God. Not that you wish others to reach for less, but for you, nothing but God's fullest blessing will do. When you stand before Him to give your accounting, your deepest longing is to hear, "Well done!"

God really does have unclaimed blessings waiting for you, my friend. I know it sounds impossible—even embarrassingly suspicious in our self-serving day. Yet that very exchange—your want for God's plenty—has been His loving will for your life from eternity past. And with a handful of core commitments on your part, you can proceed from this day forward with the confidence and expectation that your heavenly Father will bring it to pass for you.

Think of it this way: Instead of standing near the river's edge, asking for a cup of water to get you through each day, you'll do something unthinkable—you will take the little prayer with the giant prize and *jump into the river!* At that moment, you will begin to let the loving currents of God's grace and power carry you along. God's great plan for you will surround you and sweep you forward into the profoundly important and satisfying life He has waiting.

If that is what you want, keep reading.

2

So Why
Not Ask?

Oh, that you would bless me indeed!

You're at a spiritual retreat in the mountains with others who want to experience a fuller Christian life. For the duration of the retreat everyone has been matched with a mentor. Yours is in his seventies, and he's been touching lives for God longer than you've been alive.

On the way to the showers the first morning, you walk past his room. His door is ajar, and he has just knelt down to pray. You can't resist. *How exactly does a giant of the faith begin his prayers?* you wonder.

You pause and lean closer. Will he pray for revival? Pray for the hungry around the world? Pray for you?

But this is what you hear: "O Lord, I beg you first and most this morning, please bless…*me!*"

Startled at such a selfish prayer, you pad down the hall to your shower. But as you're adjusting the water

So Why Not Ask?

temperature, a thought hits you. It's so obvious, you can't believe you haven't thought it before:

Great men of the faith think differently than the rest of us.

By the time you're dressed and heading for breakfast, you're sure of it. The reason some men and women of faith rise above the rest, you decide, is that they think and pray differently than those around them.

> *Is it possible that God wants you to be more "selfish" in your prayers?*

Is it possible that God wants you to be "selfish" in your prayers? To ask for more—and more again—from your Lord? I've met so many earnest Christians who take it as a sign of immaturity to think such thoughts. They assume they'll seem impolite or greedy if they ask God for too many blessings.

Maybe you think like that. If you do, I want to show you that such a prayer is not the self-centered act it might appear, but a supremely spiritual one and exactly the kind of request our Father longs to hear.

First, let's take a closer look at Jabez's story.

Not Pain, but Gain

As far as we can tell, Jabez lived in southern Israel after the conquest of Canaan and during the time of the judges. He was born into the tribe of Judah and eventually became the notable head of a clan. Yet his story really begins with his name: "His mother called his name Jabez, saying, 'Because I bore him in pain.'"

In Hebrew, the word *Jabez* means "pain." A literal rendering could read, "He causes (or will cause) pain."

Doesn't sound like the start of a promising life, does it?

He grew up with a name any boy would love to hate.

All babies arrive with a certain amount of pain, but something about Jabez's birth went beyond the usual—so much so that his mother chose to memorialize it in her son's name. Why? The pregnancy or the delivery may have been traumatic. Perhaps the baby was born breech. Or perhaps the mother's pain was emotional—maybe the child's father abandoned her during the pregnancy; maybe he had died; maybe the family had fallen into such financial straits that the prospect of another mouth to feed brought only fear and worry.

Only God knows for sure what caused the pain of this anguished mother. Not that it made much difference to young Jabez. He grew up with a name any boy would love to hate. Imagine if you had to go through childhood enduring the teasing of bullies, the daily reminders of your unwelcome arrival, and mocking questions like, "So, young man, what *was* your mother thinking?"

Yet by far the heaviest burden of Jabez's name was how it defined his future. In Bible times, a man and his name were so intimately related that "to cut off the name" of an individual amounted to the same thing as killing him. A name was often taken as a wish for or prophecy about the child's future. For example, Jacob can mean "grabber," a good one-word biography for that scheming patriarch. Naomi and her husband named their two sons Mahlon and Chilion. Translation? "Puny" and "pining." And that was exactly what they were. Both of them died in early adulthood. Solomon means "peace," and sure enough, he became the first king of Israel to reign without going to war. A name that meant "pain" didn't bode well for Jabez's future.

Despite his dismal prospects, Jabez found a way

out. He had grown up hearing about the God of Israel who had freed his forefathers from slavery, rescued them from powerful enemies, and established them in a land of plenty. By the time he was an adult, Jabez believed and fervently hoped in this God of miracles and new beginnings.

> *When we ask God's blessing, we're not asking for more of what we could get for ourselves.*

So why not ask for one?

That's what he did. He prayed the biggest, most improbable request imaginable:

"Oh, that You would bless me *indeed*...!"

I love the urgency, the personal vulnerability of his plea. In Hebrew, adding "indeed" to this prayer was like adding five exclamation points, or writing the request in capital letters and underlining it.

In my mind's eye, I picture Jabez standing before a massive gate recessed into a sky-high wall. Weighed down by the sorrow of his past and the dreariness of his present, he sees before him only impossibility—a future shut off. But raising his hands to heaven, he cries out, "Father, oh, Father! Please bless me! And what I really mean is...bless me a lot!"

So Why Not Ask?

With the last word, the transformation begins. He hears a tremendous crack. Then a groan. Then a rumble as the huge gate swings away from him in a wide arc. There, stretching to the horizon, are fields of blessings.

And Jabez steps forward into another life.

BLESSING IS NOT ABOUT SNEEZING

Before we can ask for God's blessing with confidence, we need a clear understanding of what the word means. We hear "bless" or "blessing" intoned from every pulpit. We ask God to bless the missionaries, the kids, and the food we're about to eat. It's something Grandma says when she hears you sneeze.

No wonder the meaning of blessing gets watered down to something vague and innocuous like "Have a nice day." No wonder so many Christians aren't as desperate as Jabez was to receive it!

To bless in the biblical sense means to ask for or to impart supernatural favor. When we ask for God's blessing, we're not asking for more of what we could get for ourselves. We're crying out for the wonderful, unlimited goodness that only God has the power to know about or give to us. This kind of richness is what the writer was referring to in Proverbs: "The Lord's blessing is our greatest wealth; all our work adds nothing to it" (Proverbs 10:22, TLB).

Notice a radical aspect of Jabez's request for blessing: *He left it entirely up to God to decide what the blessings would be and where, when, and how Jabez would receive them.* This kind of radical trust in God's good intentions toward us has nothing in common with the popular gospel that you should ask God for a Cadillac, a six-figure income, or some other material sign that you have found a way to cash in on your connection with Him. Instead, the Jabez blessing focuses like a laser on our wanting for ourselves nothing more and nothing less than what God wants for us.

When we seek God's blessing as the ultimate value in life, we are throwing ourselves entirely into the river of His will and power and purposes for us. All our other needs become secondary to what we really want—which is to become wholly immersed in what God is trying to do in us, through us, and around us for His glory.

Let me tell you a guaranteed by-product of sincerely seeking His blessing: Your life will become marked by miracles. How do I know? Because He promises it, and I've seen it happen in my own! God's power to accomplish great things suddenly finds no obstruction in you. You're moving in His direction. You're praying for exactly what God desires. Suddenly the unhindered forces of heaven can begin to accomplish God's perfect will—through you. And you will be the first to notice!

But there's a catch.

Mr. Jones Goes to Heaven

What if you found out that God had it in mind to send you twenty-three specific blessings today, but you got only one? What do you suppose the reason would be?

There's a little fable about a Mr. Jones who dies and goes to heaven. Peter is waiting at the gates to give him a tour. Amid the splendor of golden streets, beautiful mansions, and choirs of angels that Peter shows him, Mr. Jones notices an odd-looking building. He thinks it looks like an enormous warehouse—it has no windows and only one door. But when he asks to see inside, Peter hesitates. "You really don't want to see what's in there," he tells the new arrival.

Why would there be any secrets in heaven? Jones wonders. *What incredible surprise could be waiting for me in there?* When the official tour is over he's still wondering, so he asks again to see inside the structure.

Finally Peter relents. When the apostle opens the door, Mr. Jones almost knocks him over in his haste to enter. It turns out that the enormous building is filled with row after row of shelves, floor to ceiling, each stacked neatly with white boxes tied in red ribbons.

"These boxes all have names on them," Mr. Jones muses aloud. Then turning to Peter he asks, "Do I have one?"

"Yes, you do." Peter tries to guide Mr. Jones back outside. "Frankly," Peter says, "if I were you...." But Mr. Jones is already dashing toward the "J" aisle to find his box.

Peter follows, shaking his head. He catches up with Mr. Jones just as he is slipping the red ribbon off his box and popping the lid. Looking inside, Jones has a moment of instant recognition, and he lets out a deep sigh like the ones Peter has heard so many times before.

Because there in Mr. Jones's white box are all the blessings that God wanted to give to him while he was on earth...but Mr. Jones had never asked.

"Ask," promised Jesus, "and it will be given to you" (Matthew 7:7). "You do not have because you do not ask," said James (James 4:2). Even though there is no limit to God's goodness, if you didn't ask Him for a blessing yesterday, you didn't get all that you were supposed to have.

That's the catch—if you don't ask for His blessing, you forfeit those that come to you only when you ask. In the same way that a father is honored to have a child beg for his blessing, your Father is delighted to respond generously when His blessing is what you covet most.

GOD'S NATURE IS TO BLESS

Perhaps you think that your name is just another word for pain or trouble, or that the legacy you have been handed from your family circumstances is nothing but a liability. You just don't feel like a candidate for blessing.

Or perhaps you're one of those Christians who thinks that once you're saved, God's blessings sort of drizzle over your life at a predetermined rate, no matter what you do. No extra effort required.

Or perhaps you have slipped into a ledger-keeping mindset with God. In your blessings account you have a column for deposits and one for withdrawals. Has God been unusually kind to you lately? Then you think that you shouldn't expect, much less ask for, Him to credit your account. You might even think He should ignore you for a while, or even debit your account by sending some trouble your way.

> *I'm asking you to change the way you think.*

This kind of thinking is a sin and a trap! When Moses said to God on Mount Sinai, "Show me Your glory" (Exodus 33:18), he was asking for a more intimate understanding of God. In response, God described Himself as "the Lord, the Lord God, merciful and gracious, longsuffering, and abounding in goodness and truth" (34:6).

Incredible! The very nature of God is to have goodness in so much abundance that it overflows into

So Why Not Ask?

our unworthy lives. If you think about God in any other way than that, I'm asking you to change the way you think. Why not make it a lifelong commitment to ask God every day to bless you—and while He's at it, bless you *a lot?*

God's bounty is limited only by us, not by His resources, power, or willingness to give. Jabez was blessed simply because he refused to let any obstacle, person, or opinion loom larger than God's nature. And God's nature is to bless.

His kindness in recording Jabez's story in the Bible is proof that it's not who you are, or what your parents decided for you, or what you were "fated" to be that counts. What counts is knowing who you want to be and asking for it.

Through a simple, believing prayer, you can change your future. You can change what happens one minute from now.

3

LIVING LARGE
FOR GOD

Oh, that You would enlarge my territory!

The next part of the Jabez prayer—a plea for more territory—is where you ask God to enlarge your life so you can make a greater impact for Him.

From both the context and the results of Jabez's prayer, we can see that there was more to his request than a simple desire for more real estate. He wanted more influence, more responsibility, and more opportunity *to make a mark for the God of Israel.*

Depending on the version you're reading, the word *territory* can also be translated *coast* or *borders*. For Jabez and his contemporaries, that word carried the same emotional power as the words *homestead* or *frontier* did for generations of American pioneers. It spoke of a place of one's own with plenty of room to grow.

Living Large for God

In Jabez's time part of Israel's recent national history was Joshua's conquest of Canaan and the partitioning of the Promised Land into chunks of real estate for each tribe. When Jabez cried out to God, "Enlarge my territory!" he was looking at his present circumstances and concluding, "Surely I was born for more than this!" As a farmer or herdsman, he looked over the spread his family had passed down to him, ran his eye down the fence lines, visited the boundary markers, calculated the potential—and made a decision: *Everything you've put under my care, O Lord—take it, and enlarge it.*

> *He looked at his circumstances and concluded, "Surely I was born for more than this!"*

If Jabez had worked on Wall Street, he might have prayed, "Lord, increase the value of my investment portfolios." When I talk to presidents of companies, I often talk to them about this particular mind-set. When Christian executives ask me, "Is it right for me to ask God for more business?" my response is, "Absolutely!" If you're doing your business God's way, it's not only right to ask for more, but He is waiting for you to ask. Your business is the territory God has entrusted to you.

He wants you to accept it as a significant opportunity to touch individual lives, the business community, and the larger world for His glory. Asking Him to enlarge that opportunity brings Him only delight.

Suppose Jabez had been a wife and a mother. Then the prayer might have gone: "Lord, add to my family, favor my key relationships, multiply for Your glory the influence of my household." Your home is the single most powerful arena on earth to change a life for God. Why wouldn't He want you to be mighty for Him?

No matter what your vocation, the highest form of Jabez's prayer for more territory might sound something like:

O God and King, please expand my opportunities and my impact in such a way that I touch more lives for Your glory. Let me do more for You!

When you pray like this, things get pretty exciting.

Moving the Boundary Lines

During a weeklong speaking engagement some years ago at a large Christian college in California, I chal-

Living Large for God

lenged students to pray the Jabez prayer for more blessing and greater influence. I suggested that the 2000-member student body set a ministry goal worthy of a college of its stature.

"Why not look at the globe and pick an island," I suggested. "When you have it picked out, put together a team of students, charter an airliner, then take over the island for God."

Some students roared. Some questioned my sanity. But nearly everyone listened. I persisted. I had been to the island of Trinidad and seen the need, I told them. "You should ask God for Trinidad," I said. "And a DC-10."

I had no immediate takers.

Still, the challenge prompted a flurry of stimulating conversations. I found most students eager to do something meaningful with their time and talents, but unsure where to start. They usually made a point of listing their deficiencies in skill, money, courage, or opportunity.

"You should ask God for Trinidad," I said. "And a DC-10."

I spent much of that week asking a question: If the God of heaven loves you infinitely and wants you in

His presence every moment, and if He knows that heaven is a much better place for you, then why on earth has He left you here? With student after student, I pressed home what I understand to be a biblical answer to that question: because God wants you to be moving out your boundary lines, taking in new territory for Him—maybe an island—and reaching people in His name.

God was at work. A week after I had returned home, I received a letter from a student named Warren. He told me that he and his friend Dave had decided to challenge God's power and ask Him to bless them and enlarge their borders. Specifically, they had prayed that God would give them the opportunity to witness to the governor of the state *that weekend*. Throwing their sleeping bags in Warren's '63 Plymouth Valiant, they had driven the 400 miles to the capital to pound on doors.

The letter continued:

By Sunday night when we got back from Sacramento, this is what had happened:

We had expressed our faith to two gas station attendants, four security guards, the head of the U.S. National Guard, the director of the Department of Health, Education, and Welfare for the state of California, the head of the California Highway Patrol, the governor's secretary, and finally the governor himself.

As God is making us grow, we are thankful and scared stiff. Thanks again for your challenge!

That was just the beginning. Over the next weeks and months, a vision for more territory swept the campus. By fall, a student team headed by Warren and Dave had mounted a major mission project for the following summer. They called it Operation Jabez. Their objective: assemble a team of self-supported student workers, charter a jet, and—you guessed it—fly to the island of Trinidad for a summer of ministry.

And that is exactly what they did. One hundred and twenty-six students and faculty signed up. By the time the jet took off fully loaded from Los Angeles, Operation Jabez boasted trained teams ready to minister through drama, construction, vacation Bible school, music, and home visitation. The college president called Operation Jabez the single most significant student ministry venture in the college's history.

Two students had asked God to enlarge their territory—and He did! One little prayer had remapped boundary lines and impacted the lives of thousands of people.

"I Think This Is My Appointment"

The Jabez prayer is a revolutionary request. Just as it is highly unusual to hear anyone pray, "God, please bless *me!*" so it is rare to hear anyone plead, "God, please give me more ministry!" Most of us think our lives are too full already. But when, in faith, you start to pray for more ministry, amazing things occur. As your opportunities expand, your ability and resources supernaturally increase, too. Right away you'll sense the pleasure God feels in your request and His urgency to accomplish great things through you.

People will show up on your doorstep or at the table next to you. They'll start saying things that surprise even them. They'll ask for something—they're not sure what—and wait for your reply.

Living Large for God

I call these encounters Jabez appointments.

I remember the first time I asked for one. It was in a very surprising place—aboard a ship off the coast of Turkey. I was traveling alone, scouting a tour company that specialized in taking groups around the Mediterranean, following in the footsteps of the early church. We had enjoyed beautiful days aboard with plenty of time for me to work on various projects, but I was getting lonelier by the day. The morning we anchored at Patmos, the island where John wrote the Book of Revelation, I hit bottom.

> *I took a table at an outdoor café and ordered a cup of coffee.*

Instead of taking the guided tour, I walked around the streets of the little port talking to the Lord. *Lord, I feel so homesick and weak,* I prayed. *But I want to be your servant. Even now, enlarge my borders. Send somebody who needs me.*

Entering a small square, I took a table at an outdoor café and ordered a cup of coffee. A few minutes later I heard a man's voice behind me. "You on the cruise ship?"

I looked up to see a young man walking toward

me. "Yes, I am," I said. "How about you?"

He said he was an American living on the island, then asked if he could join me. His name was Terry. Within minutes he was pouring out his story. As it turned out, his marriage was on the rocks. In fact, that day was the end. His wife had said she would be gone by evening.

You know what I was thinking by that time, don't you? *Okay, Lord. I think this is my appointment. And I accept....*

"Do you want your wife to leave?" I asked. He said no.

"Open to a couple of ideas?" I offered. When he said yes, I knew it was the Lord's confirmation of another Jabez experience. I spent the next hour talking through several key biblical principles for a happy marriage. Terry hadn't heard of even one before.

By the time I was done, Terry was so anxious to give his new insights a chance to save his marriage that he jumped to his feet. "Listen, Terry," I said, "I really want to hear how things go for you and your wife today. Whatever happens, come by the boat before we sail and tell me, okay?"

Terry agreed, waved, and was gone. By that evening, everyone was back on board. I walked the deck, waiting. I was still lonely, kind of frustrated, and starting to second-guess what had gone on inside Terry over coffee. When the captain ordered the final blast announcing our departure, I walked to the back of the ship where the crew was busy throwing off the stern lines. And there, running towards us along the shore, came a young couple hand in hand. When they got close enough to see me hanging over the rail, they started yelling. "It worked! It worked! We're together!"

The rest of the voyage I was so exhilarated at what God had done that I felt like I was floating without help from the ship. God had made an appointment for that young man and me. And He had been bringing us toward each other from the moment I had asked for a larger life in His service.

Living by God's Math

Whatever our gifts, education, or vocation might be, our calling is to do God's work on earth. If you want, you can call it living out your faith for others. You can call it ministry. You can call it every Christian's day job.

But whatever you call it, God is looking for people who want to do more of it, because sadly, most believers seem to shrink from living at this level of blessing and influence.

Our reluctance comes from getting our numbers right, but our arithmetic completely wrong.

For most of us, our reluctance comes from getting our numbers right, but our arithmetic completely wrong. For example, when we're deciding what size territory God has in mind for us, we keep an equation in our heart that adds up something like this:

My abilities + experience + training
+ my personality and appearance
+ my past + the expectations of others
= my assigned territory.

No matter how many sermons we've heard about God's power to work through us, we simply gloss over the meaning of that one little word *through*. Sure, we say we want God to work *through* us, but what we really mean is *by* or *in association with*. Yet God's reminder to us is the same one He gave the Jews when they returned from captivity to a decimated homeland: "Not by might nor by power but by My Spirit, says the Lord of hosts" (Zechariah 4:6).

Our God specializes in working through normal people who believe in a supernormal God who will do His work through them. What He's waiting for is the invitation. That means God's math would look more like this:

My willingness and weakness
+ God's will and supernatural power
= my expanding territory.

When you start asking in earnest—begging—for more influence and responsibility with which to honor Him, God will bring opportunities and people into your path. You can trust Him that He will never send someone to you whom you cannot help by His leading and strength. You'll nearly always feel fear when you begin to take new territory for Him, but you'll also experience the tremendous thrill of God carrying you along as you're doing it. You'll be like John and Peter, who were given the words to say at the moment they needed them.

One day in answer to Darlene's prayers for an enlarged ministry, a neighbor we hardly knew came knocking at our door. "Ma'am," she said through tears, "My husband is dying, and I have nobody to talk to. Can you help me?"

He will never send someone to you whom you cannot help.

Larger borders. An appointment to keep.

Recently on a cross-country train trip, I prayed again that God would enlarge my borders. While I was eating in the dining car, I asked the Lord to send someone who needed Him. A woman sat down across the table from me and said she needed to ask me a question. She knew my name, but little else about me. She looked deeply agitated.

"What can I do for you?" I asked.

"I'm afraid of the Antichrist," she replied. "For fifty years, I've lived in dread that I won't recognize him when he comes and that I'll be deceived by him and receive the mark of the beast."

That point-blank question from a woman I'll never

meet again led to a moving conversation and a beautiful spiritual deliverance.

Larger borders. An appointment to keep.

YOUR FRONT-ROW SEAT

To pray for larger borders is to ask for a miracle—it's that simple. A miracle is an intervention by God to make something happen that wouldn't normally happen. That, and nothing less, was what Jabez had to have to transcend his name and transform his circumstances.

Do you believe miracles still happen? Many Christians I've met do not. I remind them that miracles don't have to break natural law to be a supernatural event. When Christ stilled the storm, He didn't set aside universal law—the storm would eventually have subsided on its own. Instead, He directed the weather pattern. When Elijah prayed for it to stop raining, God directed the natural cycle of drought and rain.

In the same way, God's miracle-working powers were clearly in evidence when, knowing Terry's need, He brought us together on Patmos. And when, knowing the needs of the woman on the train, He arranged a conversation between us.

The most exhilarating miracles in my life have always started with a bold request to expand God's kingdom *a lot*. When you take little steps, you don't need God. It's when you thrust yourself in the mainstream of God's plans for this world—which are beyond our ability to accomplish—and plead with Him, *Lord, use me—give me more ministry for You!*—that you release miracles. At that moment, heaven sends angels, resources, strength, and the people you need. I've seen it happen hundreds of times.

God always intervenes when you put His agenda before yours and go for it! Amazingly, if you have prayed to the Lord to expand a border, you *will* recognize His divine answer. You'll have a front-row seat in a life of miracles.

4

THE TOUCH
OF GREATNESS

Oh, that Your hand would be with me!

Now you've done it. Gone over the edge. Gotten in too deep. Come up smack against the cold stone of reality. You are unable to hold on to the life you reached for….

Having dared to ask for an enlarged ministry, more than a few Christians have faltered at this point in their spiritual transformation. They've received blessings on a scale they hadn't imagined possible. They've seen God stretch the limits of their influence and opportunities.

But suddenly the rush of wind under their wings stops. Helpless, they start to plummet.

Sound familiar? Maybe your new business opportunities threaten to outrun your experience and resources. Maybe the teenagers who have started congregating in your kitchen suddenly seem to be influencing your family more negatively than you are influencing them positively. Maybe the new ministry opportunities you prayed for and received are turning out to require a person with much more ability than you will ever have.

You have taken up an armload of God's blessings, marched into new territory...and stumbled into overwhelming circumstances. When believers find themselves in this kind of unexpected quandary, they often feel afraid. Misled. Abandoned. A little angry.

I did....

Descending to Power

Talk about plummeting! I felt out of control and weak—nothing like a leader is supposed to feel—and most days all I could see was the ground rushing up at me. It was early in my ministry adventure, after doors had started to burst open on exciting new possibilities at Walk Thru the Bible. But I just couldn't shake the feeling that I was the wrong man for the job.

Extremely upset, I decided to seek the counsel of a trusted older man. John Mitchell was in his eighties then—a Yorkshire-born Bible teacher who had been a spiritual father to thousands. I told him what I thought God was calling me to do and then confessed my problem. I was still trying to describe my crisis in some detail when he broke in.

"Son," he said, in his kindly brogue, "that feeling you are running from is called dependence. It means you're walking with the Lord Jesus." He paused to let me take in his words, then continued. "Actually, the second you're not feeling dependent is the second you've backed away from truly living by faith."

I just couldn't shake the feeling that I was the wrong man for the job.

I didn't like what I heard. "You're saying, Dr. Mitchell, that feeling that I just can't do it is what I'm *supposed* to be feeling?"

"Why certainly, young man!" he said, beaming. "That's the one all right."

It's a frightening and utterly exhilarating truth, isn't it? As God's chosen, blessed sons and daughters, we are expected to attempt something large enough that failure is guaranteed...unless God steps in. Take a minute to prayerfully try to comprehend how contrary that truth is to everything you would humanly choose:

- It goes against common sense.
- It contradicts your previous life experience.
- It seems to disregard your feelings, training, and need for security.
- It sets you up to look like a fool and a loser.

Yet it is God's plan for His most-honored servants.

I'll admit, big-screen heroes don't seem to put any stock in dependence—but you and I were made for it. Dependence upon God makes heroes of ordinary people like Jabez and you and me. How? We're forced to cry out with Jabez's third desperate plea:

"Oh, that Your hand would be with me!"

With that, we release God's power to accomplish His will and bring Him glory through all those seeming impossibilities.

Notice that Jabez did not begin his prayer by asking for God's hand to be with him. At that point, he didn't sense the need. Things were still manageable. His risks, and the fears that go with them, were minimal. But when his boundaries got moved out, and the kingdom-sized tasks of God's agenda started coming at him, Jabez knew he needed a divine hand—and fast. He could have turned back, or he could have tried to keep going in his own strength. Instead, he prayed.

If seeking God's blessings is our ultimate act of worship, and asking to do more for Him is our utmost ambition, then asking for God's hand upon us is our strategic choice to sustain and continue the great things that God has begun in our lives.

You could call God's hand on you "the touch of greatness." You do not become great; He becomes great through you.

That's why you could call God's hand on you "the touch of greatness." You do not become great; you become dependent on the strong hand of God. Your surrendered need turns into His unlimited opportunity. And He becomes great through you.

A Ladder to the Clouds

One day when our kids were preschoolers, Darlene and I found ourselves with them at a large city park in southern California. It was the kind of park that makes a grown man wish he were a kid again. It had swings, monkey bars, and seesaws, but what was most enticing were the slides—not just one slide, but three—from small, to medium, to enormous. David, who was five at the time, took off like a shot for the small slide.

"Why don't you go down with him?" Darlene suggested.

> *He peered up the ladder. In his young imagination, it must have reached to the clouds.*

But I had another idea. "Let's wait and see what happens," I said. So we relaxed on a nearby bench and watched. David clambered happily to the top of the smallest slide. He waved over at us with a big smile, then whizzed down.

Without hesitation he moved over to the medium-sized slide. He had climbed halfway up the ladder when he turned and looked at me. I looked away. He pondered his options for a moment, then carefully backed down one step at a time.

"Honey, you ought to go help him out," my wife said.

"Not yet," I replied, hoping the twinkle in my eye

would reassure her that I wasn't just being careless.

David spent a few minutes at the bottom of the middle slide watching other kids climb up, whiz down, and run around to do it again. Finally his little mind was made up. He could do it. He climbed up...and slid down. Three times, in fact, without even looking at us.

Then we watched him turn and head toward the highest slide. Now Darlene was getting anxious. "Bruce, I don't think he should do that by himself. Do you?"

"No," I replied as calmly as possible. "But I don't think he will. Let's see what he does."

When David reached the bottom of the giant slide, he turned and called out, "Daddy!" But I glanced away again, pretending I couldn't hear him.

He peered up the ladder. In his young imagination, it must have reached to the clouds. He watched a teenage boy go hurtling down the slide. Then, against all odds, he decided to try. Step-by-step, hand over hand, he inched up the ladder. He hadn't reached a third of the way when he froze. By this time, the teenager was coming up behind him and yelled at him to get going. But David couldn't. He couldn't go up or down. He had reached the point of certain failure.

I rushed over. "Are you okay, son?" I asked from the bottom of the ladder.

He looked down at me, shaken but clinging to that ladder with steely determination. And I could tell he had a question ready.

"Dad, will you come down the slide with me?" he asked. The teenager was losing patience, but I wasn't about to let the moment go.

"Why, son?" I asked, peering up into his little face.

"I can't do it without you, Dad," he said, trembling. "It's too big for me!"

I stretched as high as I could to reach him and lifted him into my arms. Then we climbed that long ladder up to the clouds together. At the top, I put my son between my legs and wrapped my arms around him. Then we went zipping down the slide together, laughing all the way.

His Hand, His Spirit

That is what your Father's hand is like. You tell Him, "Father, please do this in me because I can't do it alone!

It's too big for me!" And you step out in faith to do and say things that could only come from His hand. Afterwards, your spirit is shouting, *God did that, nobody else! God carried me, gave me the words, gave me the power—and it is wonderful!*

I couldn't recommend more highly living in this supernatural dimension!

God's power under us, in us, surging through us is exactly what turns dependence into unforgettable experiences of completeness. "Not that we are sufficient of ourselves," wrote Paul, "to think of anything as being from ourselves, but our sufficiency is from God, who also made us sufficient as ministers of the new covenant" (2 Corinthians 3:5–6).

Tragic as it might sound, the hand of the Lord is so seldom experienced by even mature Christians that they don't miss it and don't ask for it. They hardly know it exists. They think of it as something reserved for prophets and apostles, but not for them. As you'd expect, when these believers arrive at points of certain failure, they tend to come to the wrong conclusion: *I've gone too far; I've ended up in the wrong place. And since I already have all the resources I'm going to get, I need to exit fast!*

Jabez, by contrast, was so certain that God's hand upon him was necessary for blessing that he couldn't imagine a life of honor without it. Let's look more closely at the meaning of his prayer.

The "hand of the Lord" is a biblical term for God's power and presence in the lives of His people (see Joshua 4:24 and Isaiah 59:1). In Acts, the phenomenal success of the early church was attributed to one thing: "The hand of the Lord was with them, and a great number believed and turned to the Lord" (Acts 11:21). A more specific New Testament description for God's hand is "the filling of the Holy Spirit." The church's growth bears powerful witness to both the necessity and availability of the hand of God to accomplish the business of God.

Consider the natural progression from more blessing to more territory to the need for supernatural power. When Jesus gave His disciples the Great Commission—"Go therefore and make disciples of all the nations…and lo, I am with you always" (Matthew 28:19–20)—He was bestowing on them both an incredible blessing and an impossible task. Into *all* the world and preach? Certainly a disaster in the making!

After all, He was commissioning such unreliable cowards as Peter, who had already proved that a girl by a campfire could get him to deny he'd ever heard of Jesus!

Yet when He sent the Holy Spirit (Acts 1:8), Jesus touched these ordinary believers with greatness, filling them with His miraculous power to spread the Gospel. In fact, you'll notice in Luke's account that the phrase "filled with the Spirit" is often linked to a consequence: They "spoke with boldness" (see Acts 4:13; 5:29; 7:51; 9:27). Only God at work *through them* could account for the miracles and mass conversions that followed.

When we ask for God's mighty presence like Jabez and the early church did, we will also see tremendous results that can be explained only as from the hand of God.

What strikes me about the early church was that believers continually sought to be filled by God (see Acts 4:23–31). They were known as a community who spent hours and even days in prayer together, waiting upon God and asking for His power (see Acts 2:42–47). They were longing to receive more of God's "hand"—a fresh spiritual in-filling of God's power that would turn impending, certain failure into a miracle and make their extraordinary assignment possible.

Paul told the Christians at Ephesus to make it a priority to be "filled with all the fullness of God" (Ephesians 3:19). To that end, he prayed that God would bless and strengthen them "with might through His Spirit" (3:16).

When was the last time your church got together and pleaded for the filling of the Spirit? When was the last time you petitioned God regularly and fervently, "Oh, put Your hand upon me! Fill me with Your Spirit!"? The rapid spread of the Good News in the Roman world couldn't have happened any other way.

Twelve Teens and a Disappearing Egg

Many years ago, while I was serving as a youth pastor at a large church in New Jersey, twelve high school kids proved to me that the hand of God is available to every believer who asks. For a summer ministry project we had prayerfully set our sights on suburban Long Island, New York. Objective: to evangelize the youth of the area in six weeks.

We decided on a three-part strategy. We would begin with backyard Bible studies, switch to beach evangelism in the afternoon, and then wrap it up with an evening outreach through local churches. Sounds simple, but I don't have to tell you that the team—youth pastor included—felt overwhelmed by the size of the task.

We invited a specialist in children's ministry on Long Island to give us some training. He told our missionary band that getting thirteen or fourteen kids in a backyard club would be a smashing success. After he left, I quietly said, "If we don't have one hundred kids in each club by the end of the week, we should consider it a failure."

Parents kept telling us that what we were attempting was impossible.

Suddenly, all of us wanted to get down on our knees and pray.

I'll never forget those young, earnest prayers. "Lord, please bless us!" and "Lord, I know it's way over my head, but please, give me a hundred kids!" and "Lord, by Your Spirit, pull off something great for Your glory!"

Parents kept telling our team that what we were attempting was impossible. And I'm sure they were right. But it started happening. Four of the six teams had more than a hundred children crammed into their meetings that first week. Some groups had to move to homes where two backyards adjoined without fences so all the kids could fit. By week's end we had shared the Good News with more than five hundred children, most of whom had never been to church.

If that wasn't enough miracles, the beach phase of our mission to Long Island brought more—helped along by a little magic. Actually, I went into a local novelty shop and came back to the group with a beginner's magic kit. You know, "everything you need to amaze and impress your friends." I stayed up until 3:00 A.M. learning how to make an egg "disappear." By the next afternoon, we were unrolling our free magic show in the sand and pleading with God for His hand to be upon us.

Specifically, we were asking the Lord for thirty decisions for salvation *by the end of the first day.*

Our audience grew from a single row of squirming children (dropped off by parents who wanted a few minutes of peace) to more than 150 bathing-suited customers. We rotated the entertainment from magic shows to storytelling to Gospel presentations. Parents began edging closer. Finally clusters of teenagers started swelling our crowd. By the end of the afternoon we had reached a count of 250. And when we finally gave an invitation, no fewer than thirty people indicated they wanted to accept Jesus Christ as their Savior—right there on the beach.

Once we had established our beach ministry, we added evening crusades for youth in local churches. God blessed our efforts beyond anyone's expectation— but right in line with the scope of our Jabez prayer. By the end of our six-week invasion, we could count twelve hundred new believers on Long Island, all of whom received helps and follow-up material.

Those twelve high school kids returned to their comfortable, middle-class lives in the suburbs convinced that *God can do anything*. The first thing that changed was their home church because they decided to pray for the Holy Spirit to move in their own congregation and bring repentance and revival.

Impossible? Not at all. Twelve kids and a youth

sponsor watched as God's hand moved through the church. As the members of the mission team shared their stories and challenged the church to ask God for more, revival swept through that church like no one could remember.

All because twelve students asked for blessings indeed, for more territory for God's glory, and for His hand of power to be upon them.

A FATHER'S TOUCH

Like any loving dad at the playground, God is watching and waiting for you to ask for the supernatural power He offers. "For the eyes of the LORD run to and fro throughout the whole earth, to show Himself strong on behalf of those whose heart is loyal to Him" (2 Chronicles 16:9). Notice that our God is not scanning the horizon for spiritual giants or seminary standouts. He eagerly seeks those who are sincerely loyal to Him. Your loyal heart is the only part of His expansion plan that He will not provide.

God is watching and waiting for you to ask.

You and I are always only one plea away from

inexplicable, Spirit-enabled exploits. By His touch you can experience supernatural enthusiasm, boldness, and power. It's up to you.

Ask every day for the Father's touch.

Because for the Christian, dependence is just another word for power.

KEEPING THE
LEGACY SAFE

Oh, that you would keep me from evil!

A full-page magazine ad depicts a Roman gladiator in big trouble. Somehow, he has dropped his sword. The enraged lion, seeing its opportunity, is in mid-lunge, jaws wide. The crowd in the Colosseum is on its feet, watching in horror as the panic-stricken gladiator tries to flee. The caption reads: *Sometimes you can afford to come in second. Sometimes you can't.*

After asking for and receiving supernatural blessing, influence, and power, Jabez might have believed that he could jump into any ring with any lion—and win. You would think that a person with the hand of God upon him would pray, "Keep me *through* evil."

But Jabez understood what that doomed gladiator

didn't: By far our most important strategy for defeating the roaring lion is to stay out of the arena. That's why the final request of his prayer was that God would keep him out of the fight:

"Oh...keep me from evil."

Jabez's last request is a brilliant but little-understood strategy for sustaining a blessed life. After all, as your life transcends the ordinary and starts to encroach on new territory for God, guess whose turf you're invading?

In the previous chapter our prayer was for supernatural power to work through our weakness; in this one our petition is for supernatural help to protect us from Satan's proven ability to make us come in second.

His last request is a brilliant strategy for sustaining a blessed life.

THE PERILS OF SPIRITUAL SUCCESS

Without doubt, success brings with it greater opportunities for failure. Just look around at the Christian leaders who have fallen into sin, dropped out of ministry, and left in their wake untold numbers of shaken, disillusioned, and injured people. As someone once said, blessedness is the greatest of perils because "it tends to dull our keen sense of dependence on God and make us prone to presumption."

The further along in a life of supernatural service you get, the more you'll need the final plea of Jabez's prayer. You are going to experience more attacks on you and your family. You are going to become familiar with the enemy's unwelcome barbs—distraction, opposition, and oppression, for starters. In fact, if your experience is anything *but* that, be concerned.

I'll never forget overhearing a conversation in seminary between a fellow student and my mentor, Professor Howard Hendricks. The student was excited to tell Dr. Hendricks how well his life was going.

"When I first came here," he said, "I was so tempted and tested I could barely keep my head above water. But now—praise God!—my life at seminary has smoothed out. I'm not being tempted hardly at all!"

But Hendricks looked deeply alarmed—not the reaction the student was expecting. "That's about the worst thing I could have heard," he told the surprised senior. "That shows me that you're no longer in the battle! Satan isn't worried about you anymore."

We were redeemed and commissioned for the front lines. That's why praying to be kept from evil is such a vital part of the blessed life.

Along with many others, I've discovered that the one time I'm particularly in need of this part of Jabez's prayer is when I have just experienced a spiritual success. Paradoxically, that's when I'm most inclined to hold a wrong (and dangerous) view of my strengths.

Years ago, a cab had picked me up in downtown Chicago and was whisking me down the Kennedy Expressway toward the airport. I slumped in the backseat, exhausted from a week of special meetings at Moody Bible Institute. God had moved in remarkable ways. I had preached every day and counseled scores of students—seventy-six, to be exact (I kept a log). Now heading home, I was physically and spiritually spent. Staring blankly out at the traffic, I reached for the Jabez prayer.

Things quickly got worse. The man on my left pulled out a pornographic magazine.

"O Lord," I pleaded, *"I have no resistance left. I'm completely worn out in Your service. I can't cope with temptation.*

Please, keep evil far from me today."

When I boarded the plane, I found I'd been assigned a middle seat—not a good start for my flight. And things quickly got worse. The man on my left pulled out a pornographic magazine. *"Lord, I thought we had a deal here!"* I groaned in my spirit, and I looked the other way. But before the plane lifted off, the man on my right opened his briefcase and pulled out his own skin magazine.

At that moment, I didn't have it in me to ask them to change their reading material. I closed my eyes. *"Lord,"* I prayed, *"I can't cope with this today. Please chase evil far away!"*

Suddenly the man on my right swore, folded up his magazine, and put it away. I looked at him to see what had prompted his action. Nothing, as far as I could tell. Then the man on the left looked at him, swore loudly, and closed up his magazine, too. Again, I could find no apparent reason for his decision.

We were over Indiana when I began laughing uncontrollably. They both asked me what was so funny.

"Gentlemen," I said, "you wouldn't believe me if I told you!"

Keeping the Legacy Safe

Playing Keep Away

We've arrived at one of Satan's hidden strongholds in believers' lives. In my experience, most Christians seem to pray solely for strength to endure temptations—for victory over the attacks of our raging adversary, Satan.

> *The most effective war against sin is to pray that we will not have to fight.*

Somehow we don't think to ask God simply to keep us away from temptation and keep the devil at bay in our lives.

But in the model prayer Jesus gave his followers, nearly a quarter of its fifty words ask for deliverance: "And do not lead us into temptation, but deliver us from the evil one" (Matthew 6:13). Nothing about spiritual insight or special powers. Not a word about confrontation.

When was the last time you asked God to keep you away from temptation? In the same way that God *wants* you to ask for more blessing, more territory, and more power, He longs to hear you plead for safekeeping from evil.

Without a temptation, we would not sin. Most of

us face too many temptations—and therefore sin too often—because we don't ask God to lead us away from temptation. We make a huge spiritual leap forward, therefore, when we begin to focus less on beating temptation and more on avoiding it.

With all the legions of heaven at His disposal, even Jesus prayed for deliverance. Even with all His divine insight, when He was tempted in the wilderness, He refused to engage Satan in a discussion about his enticing offers.

As we move deeper into the realm of the miraculous, the most effective war against sin that we can wage is to pray that we will not have to fight unnecessary temptation. And God offers us His supernatural power to do just that.

Dropping Our Weapons

The arena of temptation is usually enemy territory. By this, I don't mean that being tempted is the same thing as sinning—that's another of Satan's deceptions. What I mean is that we're usually asked to duke it out with evil in the spheres of our subjective experience. This isn't neutral ground, because we're fallen creatures with limited understandings, as Satan well knows. Here, even our finest weapons (humanly speaking) can quickly become our undoing.

Take our wisdom. It works sporadically at best because the nature of evil is to deceive us with a little bit of the truth—not all of it, mind you, but just enough to trick us. Adam and Eve weren't any more prone to succumb to temptation than we are. In fact, unlike us, they were perfect in every way, and none of their genuine needs were unmet. Satan approached the human race at its peak of promise and performance—and crushed us with one friendly conversation.

That's why, like Jabez, we should pray for protection from deception:

> *Lord, keep me from making the mistakes I'm most prone to when temptation comes. I confess that what I think is necessary, smart, or personally beneficial is so often only the beautiful wrapping on sin. So please, keep evil far from me!*

Take our experience. The further we move into new territory for Christ, the less protected are our flanks from Satan's attacks. Someone has said, "Your danger is not in being on the edge of a precipice, but in being unwatchful there." A tiny indulgence of pride or self-confidence can spell disaster. The deepest grief I've seen in fellow believers is among those who have experienced extraordinary blessings, territory, and power… only to slip into serious sin.

Like Jabez, then, we should ask to be spared dangerous misjudgments:

Lord, keep me safe from the pain and grief that sin brings. For the dangers that I can't see, or the ones that I think I can risk because of my experience (pride and carelessness), put up a supernatural barrier. Protect me, Father, by your power!

Take our feelings. Do we really understand how far the American Dream is from God's dream for us? We're steeped in a culture that worships freedom, independence, personal rights, and the pursuit of pleasure. We respect people who sacrifice to get what they want. But to be a living sacrifice? To be crucified to self?

Like Jabez, we should plead to be kept from the

Keeping the Legacy Safe

powerful pull of what feels right to us but is wrong:

Lord, keep me safe from temptations that pull at my emotions and my physical needs, that call out to my sense of what I deserve, what I have the "right" to feel and enjoy. Because You are the true source of all that is really life, direct my steps away from all that is not of You.

These are petitions for deliverance that our Father loves to hear—and answer.

WITNESS TO FREEDOM

Since Satan most opposes those who are becoming the greatest threat to him and his kingdom, the more God answers your Jabez prayers, the more you should be prepared to confront spiritual attack.

Sometimes, however, you cannot be kept from evil because by God's power you are attempting to launch a D-Day offensive against the darkness. At those times you can stand confidently against the enemy with what Paul calls "the weapons of our warfare" (2 Corinthians 10:4).

I remember a prayer meeting in the early years of

the Promise Keepers movement. The twenty-five members of our leadership team for the event were huddled in prayer as tens of thousands gathered in the stadium below. The opposition was so thick that we kept stumbling over our words and falling silent. Unless we could defeat Satan's oppression, we knew there would be no point in starting the program. Finally one of the team members stood up and began to attack evil with the truth.

Do we really understand how far the American Dream is from God's dream for us?

"Friends, the victory is already ours," he declared confidently while we continued to kneel. Utterly determined, he began praying the truth of God's will for that day back to God. His memorable prayer went something like this:

> *Lord, it is Your will that we seek this blessing for countless men and their families! We know that it is Your deepest desire to take more ground for the kingdom in this generation, on this day in history, in this stadium! And we thank You for what You're going to do.*

The best the rest of us could do at first was to labor along with him in prayer, casting ourselves upon the Lord to move in us and on our behalf. The heaviness we felt was almost too much to bear. But our prayer leader didn't falter:

Father, it is Your profound and immovable purpose that Your Holy Spirit be here—is here now in our midst—moving already through the rows of gathering men. You have come here to work in a supernatural dimension that even we can barely comprehend, but which we earnestly anticipate. And at Your name, Lord Jesus, every other power on earth must bow or flee.

At some point in his prayer, we broke through with God. Our desperate pleas turned to praise and worship. We knew we had been witnesses to freedom in the Spirit. We strode together out into that arena to boldly claim the bountiful results of what had already been accomplished in prayer.

A Legacy of Triumph

I think Jabez would have liked that prayer. He wanted to live free from the bondage of evil because God's trustworthy character and steadfast Word had showed him something unimaginably better.

"Stay out of the arena of temptation whenever possible," he would advise, "but never live in fear or defeat. By God's power, you can keep your legacy of blessing safe."

Do you believe that a supernatural God is going to show up to keep you from evil and protect your spiritual investment? Jabez did believe, and he acted on his belief. Thereafter his life was spared from the grief and pain that evil brings.

Paul told the Colossians that God had made them "alive together with [Christ]" and that having "disarmed principalities and powers, He made a public spectacle of them, triumphing over them in [the cross]" (Colossians 2:13, 15).

What an amazing declaration of victory! Through Christ, we can live in triumph—not in temptation or defeat. With the fourth plea of Jabez as part of our life, we are now ready to move up to a higher level of honor and exponentially expanding blessings.

Here's why: Unlike in most stock portfolios, in God's kingdom the safest investment also shows the most remarkable growth.

Welcome to God's Honor Roll

Jabez was more honorable than his brothers.

Do you think God has favorites? Certainly God makes His love available to all, and Jesus came to earth so that "whosoever" might call on His name and be saved.

But Jabez, whose prayer earned him a "more honorable" award from God, might have made the case that God does have favorites. His experience taught him that equal access to God's favor does not add up to equal reward. What happened to some of the others named along with him in Chronicles? Idbash, Hazelelponi, and Anub, for example. What honors and awards did they get from God?

Simply put, God favors those who ask. He holds back nothing from those who want and earnestly long for what He wants.

To say that you want to be "more honorable" in

God's eyes is not arrogance or self-centeredness. "More honorable" describes what God thinks; it's not credit we take for ourselves. You would be giving in to a carnal impulse if you were trying to outdo someone else, but you are living in the Spirit when you strive to receive God's highest reward. "I press toward the goal for the prize," Paul wrote in his last epistle (Philippians 3:14), and he looked forward to the day he could give an account for what he had done (2 Corinthians 5:9–10).

The sorrowful alternative does not appeal to me. I don't want to get to heaven and hear God say: "Let's look at your life, Bruce. Let me show you what I wanted for you and tried repeatedly to accomplish through you…but you wouldn't let me." What a travesty!

I've noticed that winning honor nearly always means leaving mediocre expectations and comfortable assumptions behind. But in this case it has very little to do with talent. How encouraging it is to find very few supersaints listed among those God has placed on His honor roll (Hebrews 11). They are mostly ordinary, easy-to-overlook people who had faith in an extraordinary, miraculous God and stepped out to act on that faith.

What they discovered was a life marked by God's blessings, supernatural provision, and divine leading *at the very moment they needed them.*

GOD'S HAND ON ME NOW

I think the immediacy—the "now-ness"—of serving God is one of the most exciting aspects of living for God's honor roll. You start to thrive in the present to a degree most Christians have never thought possible.

> *How would your day unfold if you believed that God wants your borders expanded at all times with every person?*

Think about it: How would your day unfold if you believed that God wants your borders expanded at all times with every person and if you were confident that God's powerful hand is directing you even as you minister?

During the past five years, I've been putting that belief to a very specific test, often with astounding results. I ask the Lord for more ministry; then, following the nudging of the Holy Spirit, I initiate a conversation with a person by asking a simple question: "How can I help you?"

Let me give you an example:

I was driving through Atlanta to the airport on my way to an important speaking engagement in North Carolina. Without warning, traffic slowed, then stopped. A major accident had blocked all lanes. When it became clear that I was going to miss my flight, I prayed, "Lord, please make my flight late so I can catch it."

The woman caught her breath, leaned against the wall, and started to talk.

When I finally arrived at the concourse for departure, I noticed scores of people milling around. Sure enough, the flight had been delayed. Humbled and thankful, I found myself wondering if God had something else in mind as well. I began to pray that the Lord would arrange an appointment for ministry.

Within moments, a well-dressed businesswoman approached, pulling her leather roller bag. When she joined the rest of us to wait for the flight, I noticed she seemed flustered.

I nodded hello, then asked, "What can I do for you?"

"What?" she said, not quite believing her ears.

I repeated my offer.

"You can't do anything for me," she said, kindly but firmly.

"Well, I believe there's something I can do for you, but I don't know what it is. But you do. My name is Bruce, by the way." Then I smiled at her and calmly asked again, "So, what can I do for you?"

> *As I look back, I see the footprints of Jabez and his little prayer.*

Friend, have you ever seen the Holy Spirit break through emotional and spiritual barriers right before your eyes? It's an experience you won't forget. The woman caught her breath, leaned against the wall, and started to talk. "Well, I'm flying home to divorce my husband," she said. "That's why I'm waiting to catch this flight."

Tears welled up in her eyes. I suggested we move to a quieter corner in the departure area, and I asked the Lord to place His protection around us and between us.

Her name was Sophie. Her perfectly tailored dress

and Italian leather accessories hid a broken person on the run from disappointment and despair. Her husband had been unfaithful to her and hurt her in other ways. Even though he wanted to make things right, she had had enough. When she got home, she would be pulling divorce papers out of her briefcase.

The gate attendant interrupted us. "Asheville, right? You're going to miss your plane." We were the last two to board. Now Sophie was agitated because our conversation would have to end, and she wasn't finished.

"The Lord will put us together," I said, not quite believing the confidence I heard in my voice.

"What do you mean?" Sophie asked.

"Well, He didn't have too much difficulty making the earth; He can get us two seats together."

But when we compared tickets, we were five rows apart. As we arrived at my seat, the man sitting in the middle seat next to Sophie heard us talking and turned around. "I hate middle seats," he said. "I'll switch so you can sit together."

Sophie sank into the seat beside me, momentarily speechless. During the flight, we talked about her options. I laid out some biblical principles and promises for her. I prayed with her. And by the time we landed in Asheville, she had broken through to forgiveness. She was still hurting, but she was at peace, determined to give her marriage the commitment it deserved.

As I look back over this divine appointment, I can see the footprints of Jabez and his little prayer:

- I asked for and expected God's blessing *for today*.
- I pleaded for more "territory" (more ministry and influence for Him) and stepped forward to receive it.
- I leaned precariously but confidently upon the Holy Spirit to guide my thoughts, words, and actions with Sophie and to work in the supernatural realm to accomplish what I could not.
- I asked God to keep evil (or in this case, even a hint of impropriety) from spoiling the blessing He desired to bring about through me.

Let me encourage you, friend, to reach boldly for the miracle. Your Father knows your gifts, your hindrances, and the condition you're in at every moment.

And He also knows something you can't possibly know—every single person who's in desperate need of receiving His touch *through you*. God will bring you to that person at exactly the right time and in the right circumstances.

And at that moment, you *will* receive power to be His witness.

The Cycle of Blessings

As you repeat the steps, you will set in motion a cycle of blessing that will keep multiplying what God is able to do in and through you. This is the exponential growth I referred to at the close of the previous chapter. You have asked for and received more blessing, more territory, more power, and more protection. But the growth curve soon starts to spike upwards.

The growth curve soon starts to spike upwards.

You don't reach the next level of blessing and stay there. You begin again—*Lord, bless me indeed! Lord, please enlarge…!* And so on. As the cycle repeats itself, you'll find that you are steadily moving into wider spheres of blessing and influence, spiraling ever outward and upward into a larger life for God.

The day will come—and come repeatedly during your life—that you will be so overwhelmed with God's graciousness that tears will stream down your face. I can remember saying to the Lord, "It's too much! Hold some of your blessings back!" If you're like many who use the Jabez prayer, including me, you'll come to times in your life when you feel so blessed that you stop praying for more, at least for a while.

The only thing that can break the cycle of abundant living is sin. Sin breaks the flow of God's power.

But I promise you that you will see a direct link: You will know beyond doubt that God has opened heaven's storehouses *because you prayed.*

I'll admit: The cycle of blessings will give your faith a good testing. Will you let God work in your life regardless of what He chooses? It will always be for your best. Will you surrender to His power and love and surprising plan for you? I hope you choose to do just that. You will experience the joy of knowing that God experiences deep pleasure and joy in *you!*

Welcome to God's Honor Roll

The only thing that can break this cycle of abundant living is sin, because sin breaks the flow of God's power. It is as if the electric lines to your house in Phoenix were severed and you were cut off from the immense power generators at Hoover Dam. All the incredible potential of the dam's turbines would be untapped, wasted, and waiting for the connection to be restored.

You should know that when you sin after experiencing the Jabez blessing, you'll experience a deeper grief over your disconnect from God than you ever thought possible. It's the pain that comes from having once tasted the exhilaration of God working in you at a higher level of fulfillment and then turning back.

I encourage you to rush back into God's presence and make things right, whatever it takes. Don't squander even for a minute the miracle that He has started in your life. Indescribable good still lies ahead for you and your family.

7

MAKING JABEZ MINE

So God granted him what he requested.

I challenge you to make the Jabez prayer for blessing part of the daily fabric of your life. To do that, I encourage you to follow unwaveringly the plan outlined here for the next thirty days. By the end of that time, you'll be noticing significant changes in your life, and the prayer will be on its way to becoming a treasured, lifelong habit.

1. Pray the Jabez prayer every morning, and keep a record of your daily prayer by marking off a calendar or a chart you make especially for the purpose.

2. Write out the prayer and tape it in your Bible, in your day-timer, on your bathroom mirror, or some other place where you'll be reminded of your new vision.

3. Reread this little book once each week during

Making Jabez Mine

the next month, asking God to show you important insights you may have missed.

4. Tell one other person of your commitment to your new prayer habit, and ask him or her to check up on you.

5. Begin to keep a record of changes in your life, especially the divine appointments and new opportunities you can relate directly to the Jabez prayer.

6. Start praying the Jabez prayer for your family, friends, and local church.

Of course, what you *know about* this or any other prayer won't get you anything. What you know about deliverance won't deliver you from anything. You can hang the Jabez prayer on the wall of every room in your house and nothing will happen. It's only what you believe will happen *and therefore do next* that will release God's power for you and bring about a life change. But when you act, you will step up to God's best for you.

I'm living proof.

> *It's only what you believe will happen and therefore do next that will bring about a life change.*

The Rest of the Story

In the first chapter of this book, I told you how choosing to pray for a larger work for God redirected the course and quality of my life. Let me tell you the rest of the story.

My wife and I took our first step to making the Jabez prayer a regular part of our spiritual journey in that yellow kitchen in Dallas with a Texas rainstorm rattling the windows. We wanted so much to reach for more—to do and become all that God had in mind for us. But we had no idea what would happen.

> *His borders encompass the whole world.*

Over the years at Walk Thru the Bible, our once feeble prayers have grown because *He has never stopped answering!* I can remember when we had twenty-five or thirty Bible conferences in a year. This year Walk Thru will conduct over twenty-five hundred Bible conferences—fifty each weekend. The ministry now publishes ten magazines each month to help individuals and families grow in God's Word every day. We recently passed the 100 million mark in total issues published.

Making Jabez Mine

I don't mention these numbers to impress you. I share this story because it is a very personal one and, to me at least, almost shocking evidence of what God's grace and Jabez praying can do.

Now God has stretched our faith yet again. Recently we found ourselves asking an entirely different question—not so much "Lord, enlarge our borders" as "Lord, what are Your borders? What do You want done?"

Obviously, His borders encompass the whole world. Clearly, it is His complete will for us to reach the world—*right now!* So our leadership team began to ask how we could be part of making that happen. Soon we decided to pray the biggest little prayer we could imagine: *O God—let us reach the whole world for You.*

> *Humanly speaking, this kind of growth is unexplainable.*

In January 1998 we began WorldTeach, birthed from the womb of the Jabez prayer. WorldTeach is an exciting fifteen-year vision to establish the largest Bible-teaching faculty in the world—120,000—a Bible teacher for every 50,000 people on earth. As I write this closing section, I'm in

India to help train Bible teachers from six nations to take the Great Commission into every village and city and nation.

Just by looking at what is happening, I can assure you that God still answers those who have a loyal heart and pray the Jabez prayer. By its second year, WorldTeach had launched in twenty-three nations—including Russia, India, South Africa, Ukraine, and Singapore—and enrolled twenty-five hundred teachers. Our target for our third year is thirty-five nations and five thousand teachers. And we are running ahead of schedule.

One national missions leader told me that WorldTeach has had the fastest launch of any Christian ministry in history. Humanly speaking, this kind of growth is unexplainable. We are only weak humans who seek to be clean and fully surrendered to our Lord, to want what He wants for His world, and to step forward in His power and protection to see it happen now.

I don't know what you call that, but I have always called it the miracle of Jabez.

Making Jabez Mine

REDEEMED FOR THIS

I've seen something amazing happen in people like you who have suspected all along that God answers courageous prayers. When the merest ray of faith shines in your spirit, the warmth of God's truth infuses you, and you instinctively want to cry out, "Oh, Lord, please…bless me!" And I see in people like you a growing excitement and an anticipation of what will happen next.

Because something always does. Your spiritual expectations undergo a radical shift, though it might be only slightly apparent to someone else. You feel renewed confidence in the present-tense power and reality of

> *You know beyond a doubt that you were redeemed for this.*

your prayers because you know you're praying in the will and pleasure of God. You sense in the deepest recesses of your being the rightness of praying like this. You know beyond a doubt that you were redeemed for this: to ask Him for the God-sized best He has in mind for you, and to ask for it with all your heart.

Join me for that transformation. You will change your legacy and bring supernatural blessings wherever you go. God will release His miraculous power in your life now. And for all eternity, He will lavish on you His honor and delight.

The Jabez Prayer

*And Jabez called on the God of Israel saying,
"Oh, that You would bless me indeed,
and enlarge my territory,
that Your hand would be with me,
and that You would keep me from evil,
that I may not cause pain!"
So God granted him what he requested.*
1 CHRONICLES 4:10 (NKJV)

Author's update, February, 2001: Many have asked for an update on our Jabez-sized goals for WorldTeach (see pages 89–90). God is hearing our prayers. We have significantly surpassed our goal for the year 2000 of growing this Bible teaching ministry to 35 nations and 5,000 teachers worldwide. A year-end tally shows that WorldTeach has now been launched in 39 nations with an astonishing 7,982 teachers! Pray for us as we ask God to expand our borders this year to 50 nations with 12,000 teachers. Thank you. *Bruce Wilkinson*

We would love to hear from you.
Read amazing testimonies on the prayer of
Jabez or submit your own story.
Visit www.prayerofjabez.com
or write Multnomah Publishers/Jabez Stories
P. O. Box 1720, Sisters, OR 97759

see next page for other Bruce Wilkinson products

More Resources to Help You Live *The Prayer of Jabez*

Introducing a new product line for Bruce Wilkinson's powerful teaching on *The Prayer of Jabez*. These resources will help you delve deeper into understanding and living out this powerful principle.

- **The Prayer of Jabez Audio** — ISBN 1-57673-842-6
- **The Prayer of Jabez Leather Edition** — ISBN 1-57673-857-4
- **The Prayer of Jabez Journal** — ISBN 1-57673-860-4
- **The Prayer of Jabez Devotional** — ISBN 1-57673-844-2
- **The Prayer of Jabez Bible Study** — ISBN 1-57673-979-1
- **The Prayer of Jabez Bible Study with Leaders Guide**
  ISBN 1-57673-980-5
- **The Prayer of Jabez for Teens** — ISBN 1-57673-815-9
- **The Prayer of Jabez Gift Edition** — ISBN 1-57673-810-8

visit www.prayerofjabez.com

Next in The BreakThrough Series

Secrets of the Vine

Dr. Bruce Wilkinson explores John 15 to show readers how to make maximum impact for God. Dr. Wilkinson demonstrates how Jesus is the Vine of life, discusses four levels of "fruit bearing" (doing the good work of God), and reveals three life-changing truths that will lead readers to new joy and effectiveness in His kingdom.

ISBN 1-57673-975-9

Also Available on Audiocassette
Read by author Bruce Wilkinson
ISBN 1-57673-977-5

More from Bruce Wilkinson

Why don't I have passion in my spiritual life?

How can I be closer to God?

Is it still possible to restore my marriage?

Can I raise my children to be "on fire" for God?

Join Dr. Bruce Wilkinson to find the answer to *your* spiritual breakthrough.

ISBN 1-57673-536-2

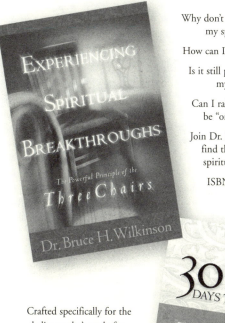

Crafted specifically for the believer who's ready for change, *30 Days* incorporates the wisdom of today's most influential Christian communicators to reveal priceless insights about life, marriage, family, and God.

ISBN 1-57673-581-8

It's Time for Your Child to Experience Life Changing Prayer

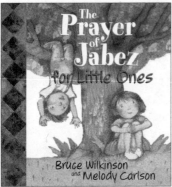

Available July 2001

The Prayer of Jabez for Little Ones
Board Book for Ages 2-5
6 X 6

We Inspire Kids

The Prayer of Jabez for Kids
Ages 8-12
4 1/2 X 6

THE BREAKTHROUGH SERIES

SECRETS *of the* VINE *for Women*

BREAKING THROUGH to ABUNDANCE

DARLENE MARIE WILKINSON

Multnomah® Publishers *Sisters, Oregon*

SECRETS OF THE VINE FOR WOMEN
published by Multnomah Publishers, Inc.
© 2003 by Exponential, Inc.

International Standard Book Number: 1-59052-156-0

Cover design by David Carlson Design
Cover image by Allen Garns

Scripture is from *The Holy Bible,* New King James Version.
Copyright © 1982 by Thomas Nelson, Inc. Used by permission.

Other Scripture quotations:
The Holy Bible, New International Version (NIV)
1973, 1984 by International Bible Society,
used by permission of Zondervan Publishing House

Multnomah is a trademark of Multnomah Publishers, Inc.,
and is registered in the U.S. Patent and Trademark Office.
The colophon is a trademark of Multnomah Publishers, Inc.

Printed in the United States of America

ALL RIGHTS RESERVED
No part of this publication may be reproduced,
stored in a retrieval system, or transmitted, in any form or by
any means—electronic, mechanical, photocopying, recording,
or otherwise—without prior written permission.

For information:
MULTNOMAH PUBLISHER, INC. • P.O. BOX 1720 •
SISTERS, OREGON 97759

03 04 05 06 07 08 09 10—8 7 6 5 4 3 2 1 0

Table of Contents

Preface: *A Place to Grow* 5

Chapter One: *A Spiritual Harvest* 7

Chapter Two: *The Touch of Abundance* 19

Chapter Three: *Lifted by Love* 33

Chapter Four: *Making Room for More* 53

Chapter Five: *The Miracle of Much Fruit* 73

Chapter Six: *Your Father's Prize* 97

Appendix: *Three Seasons in God's Vineyard* ...111

PREFACE

A Place to Grow

Dear Reader,

Thank you for picking up *Secrets of the Vine for Women*. I'm praying that you, along with thousands of others, will remember this little book as a turning point in your life.

A turning point, a pivotal experience, something that leaves you forever changed—that's what so many women are looking for today. And I can tell you from personal experience that Jesus' words in John 15 are life changing! In this conversation in a vineyard the night before He died, Jesus showed His followers how God would be at work to bring each of them to a truly abundant life.

I invite you to step with me into that vineyard and listen carefully to what Jesus said. And as you read, may you be in awe of your Father's faithfulness and greatness, because incredible spiritual abundance is His plan today for you, too.

With affection,

Darlene Marie

*"I have come that they
may have life, and that they may
have it more abundantly."*

JOHN 10:10

CHAPTER ONE

A Spiritual Harvest

The train creaked to a stop. A young woman standing ready at the door gazed out over the rooftop of the railway station to the golden hills of Tuscany. "How beautiful it is!" she sighed. The bustling cities of the north were behind her now. Finally, she was home.

Descending to the wooden platform, she felt her weariness slip away. Eagerly, she scanned the sea of faces until she saw him. Her father, a tall, bronzed man, was easy to find in a crowd, and she had sought him out many times. When she caught his eye, he rushed toward her, arms outstretched, and wrapped her in an embrace.

"Welcome, my beautiful girl!" he cried. "I've missed you so much!"

It didn't take long to have her bags sent on ahead. As usual, her father wanted to take her on foot out of the village and up the twisting lanes that led to their home. Leaving the station, they walked hand in hand, talking and laughing. He asked about her life in the city. She asked about the approaching harvest. And as they talked and walked, she reveled in the warm sun of an Italian autumn.

At the crest of the hill her eyes fell upon a familiar scene—her father's vineyard, rolling away in neatly tended rows. She had grown up following her father as he worked up and down those rows. And since childhood she'd known that her father was well-respected throughout the region as a champion vinedresser. But at her first view of the vineyard, now heavy with fruit, her breath caught in her throat.

"Papa!" she exclaimed. "I've never seen such a promising crop!" She walked down a row to look more closely. Huge clusters of dark, satiny grapes hung from every branch.

Turning back to her father, she saw the pleasure on his face. "You must be very proud," she said. "I still remember the wretched state of these plants when we first came here. How diligently you have worked all these years to produce such an incredible yield!"

She tucked her arm in his, steering them toward the house. "I'm so glad to be home to celebrate this harvest with you!" she said. This was the most anticipated season in the vineyard, and she didn't want to miss any of it. She could hardly wait.

A Spiritual Harvest

The young woman in our story has, for many years, observed the tending of her father's vineyard. She is well acquainted with all that is required to produce a harvest. And she knows how much a great harvest of prize-winning grapes will mean to her father.

You, on the other hand, may never have walked through a vineyard or even seen grapes hanging from a branch. For that reason, in the chapters to come we'll revisit our young friend and her father as the grape harvest approaches. I want you to feel the sun, smell the earth, and touch the rough leaves of the grape plant. I want you to celebrate with them as they anticipate a bumper crop.

Why should you think about grapes?

Because the truths I want to explore with you in this little book, based on Jesus' teachings in John 15, have a lot to do with grapes and how they grow. The vineyard we're interested in is a spiritual picture rather than an actual place. But I promise that the lessons you learn there will be so real to you that they will change your life forever.

I can make such a promise because our teacher is Jesus,

> *Abundance— a life as full as possible of God's best.*

and His words are part of His last conversation with His friends on the night before He died. What He said surprised His disciples. I'm sure it wasn't what they wanted to hear. But Jesus knew it was what they desperately needed to hear. Otherwise they would never experience the abundant life God had in mind for them.

Abundance—a life as full as possible of God's best. It's the picture God has in mind for us, too. Unfortunately, if we don't understand what God does to bring that wonderful harvest about, we can actually work against His good hand in our lives without ever knowing it.

But then Jesus makes a string of disturbing announcements.

By the time you finish this little book, some important principles of how abundance happens in your life will become clear, and you'll learn how to cooperate with your Father's hand—for your greatest fulfillment, and for His glory.

For example, you'll discover how He intervenes when sin is holding you back. You'll understand how He responds when your own good intentions are leading you astray. You'll learn, perhaps for the first time, just how much He longs to enjoy intimate fellowship with you, and you'll have a clear idea of what you need to do to make that relationship happen. And finally, you'll know for certain that you can expect more lasting results from your life than you ever thought possible.

Listen in now as Jesus talks quietly with His friends over dinner.

DINNER REVELATIONS

It is the night of the Passover. Jesus and His inner circle of followers are eating together in the upper room. They have much to celebrate. The events leading up to this meal have confirmed to the disciples that Jesus is the long-awaited Messiah. They're convinced that by tomorrow, if not before, Jesus will give the word and usher in His new kingdom. And it's a kingdom they can't wait to be part of.

The atmosphere is electric. But then Jesus makes a string of disturbing announcements: One of the disciples will betray Him. One will deny Him. He is leaving, and they can't follow. And the final, shattering disclosure: that "the ruler of this world is coming"—and it will not be Him.

The men are speechless. Just moments ago they were poised for a great future. Now Jesus seems to be saying that

He was thinking of His love for them. And I believe He was thinking of you.

it will never happen. All their dreams and plans have turned into a crushing disappointment.

At the end of the evening, Jesus says, "Arise, let us go from here." As He leads them out into the night, questions and doubts swirl in their minds. By the light of lamps and torches, they follow Him quietly through the winding streets of Jerusalem, down to a lower gate of the city, and out into the Kidron Valley.

Here, they walk through ancient vineyards, carefully tended for generations and famously productive. Jesus and His followers find their way through the rows of vines on their way to their destination—the Garden of Gethsemane on a nearby hill.

We anticipate a bright tomorrow, only to find ourselves peering into a dark today.

It is in this very vineyard, many scholars believe, that Jesus paused to deliver His parting message to His disciples. And here, as He so often did, Jesus used an earthy, familiar illustration to impart timeless spiritual truths. Before, He had talked about water, lambs, coins, runaway sons, and bread. This time Jesus talked about fruit. "I am the vine, you are the branches," He said (John 15:5).

As He talked, I believe He was pointing to a branch, to

leaves, to a vine. But He was looking right at His friends. With every word, He was thinking of His love for them, of the challenges they'd face, of the amazing and specific future God had in mind for each one of them.

And I believe He was thinking of you.

A Picture of His Plan

One of my favorite childhood memories is of our family working around a table over a 500-piece puzzle during the Christmas holidays. I loved sorting through my pile of pieces—blue ones, green ones, multicolored ones—trying to find a perfect fit. Piece by irregular piece, the picture slowly came to life. Of course, every once in a while I'd turn the box lid over and take a long hard look at the painting on the cover. There it was—the gorgeous finished picture we were all working toward.

That box lid was proof that no matter how stuck we were at the moment, our individual pieces were made to fit together. Eventually, we knew, we'd have spread out in front of us a grand scene—a harbor full of colorful sailing boats, maybe, or a Swiss

Every touch of His hand is intended to bring us to a place of great spiritual abundance.

mountain village. We didn't have to guess at our goal. We could see where we were supposed to end up. And we could see that it would be beautiful.

You've probably been around that table with your family many times, too. And like me, you probably can't imagine how difficult those puzzles would have been to complete without having the big picture right there at hand.

That night in the vineyard, Jesus "turned the box lid over" and showed us the big picture. He wanted us to see—no matter what circumstance we're in at the moment—what God the Father is trying to accomplish in and through us for eternity. He wanted us to know how to respond to His will. He wanted us to remember that every touch of His hand is intended to bring us to a place of great spiritual abundance.

Women consistently express a desire to go deeper.

And to accomplish all that, Jesus showed us a picture of a vineyard.

Using the illustrations of a vinedresser, a vine, a branch, and fruit, Jesus told us plainly that He wants something specific from us. And He wants it so much that He continually intervenes in our lives—sometimes even with pain—to make it happen.

A Spiritual Harvest

Maybe you can identify with what those disappointed disciples experienced that night. So many women can. We know what it's like to anticipate a bright tomorrow, only to find ourselves peering into a dark today. Things are going along according to plan, then for no apparent reason we find ourselves ambushed by confusion or pain. We wonder, *Why is this happening? Has God forgotten me? What on earth is He up to in my life?*

If you have already read *Secrets of the Vine,* you know the answer. If not, what I want to share with you may come as a surprise—yet it's a surprise full of promise. Either way, if what you want most is greater fruitfulness and service and impact for God in your life, then the teachings of the vineyard are for you.

Where Women Walk

You might be wondering why I decided to write *Secrets of the Vine for Women.* After all, *Secrets of the Vine* is already a publishing success. And it turns out that it has been even more widely read by women than men. Bruce was flooded with letters from women saying things like, "This book felt like a big hug from God," and "*Secrets* explained what I experienced just last week!" Everywhere I go I meet women who have been changed by the truths of John 15.

But in fact, the special appeal of this message for women is the very reason I feel compelled to pick up my pen (and yes, I start out by writing in longhand!). Wherever I teach on this subject, woman consistently express a desire to go deeper. They want to learn more about how Jesus' vineyard conversation applies to their experiences as women in today's world. In short, they want to continue the conversation!

And so do I.

In the pages to come I will introduce you to some women like yourself. They are mothers, daughters, wives, sisters, and singles with one thing in common: They believe God does have a loving and amazing plan for greater fruitfulness in their lives…and they want it with all their heart!

> *I realized how much I actually resisted what God was doing to help me flourish.*

The message of *Secrets of the Vine for Women* is also a very personal one for me. More than any other teaching I've explored, it has dramatically changed the way I respond to challenging circumstances in my life. I realized how much I actually resisted what God was doing to help me flourish. It wasn't until I understood what Jesus taught about God's ways with us that I went from questioning God's motives to embracing His plan for my life. The best word I can come up with for the result is *abundance*.

If that's what you want with all your heart, please join me in the pages ahead.

*"I am the true vine, and
My Father is the vinedresser."*

JOHN 15:1

CHAPTER TWO

The Touch of Abundance

While they waited for supper to be served, the young woman and her father stepped out onto the tiled courtyard. The vineyard was still visible in the dusky light. In just a few days, workers from miles around would arrive to assist with the harvest.

She watched and listened as her father pointed out various changes in the landscape before them.

"Do you remember the view from here when I bought this estate?" her father asked.

She contemplated his question. "I remember more rows of vines than I'd ever seen. And I remember leaves. I remember a lot of scraggly—"

"But do you remember grapes?" her father asked.

"Only a few, Papa. A grape here or there." She was smiling. He was smiling, too. They'd had this conversation before.

Now, gazing out across the grape-laden vines, she remembers a morning long ago . . .

She's a little girl, playing with clumps of earth as she watches her father work patiently on a branch.

Peering up at her father from under a straw hat, she exclaims, "But I don't see any grapes here, Papa. You said we were going to grow grapes!"

Her father laughs. "You have good eyes, don't you?" He straightens up to look around. "These branches don't have any fruit. Not yet. They need lots of patient care and tending. But one day, my daughter, one day. You wait and see . . ."

One thing that any gardener knows is that a bumper crop doesn't just happen. It takes a plan. It takes time, work, and plenty of close attention. The vinedresser in our story knows that. He is personally involved with each branch in his vineyard because he wants to see each branch flourish and grow.

Now listen carefully to the words of Jesus that night in the vineyard. These verses may be familiar to you. But receive them this time as a first-person description of your Father at work in His garden.

> *"I am the true vine, and My Father is the vinedresser. Every branch in Me that does*

not bear fruit He takes away; and every branch that bears fruit He prunes, that it may bear more fruit. I am the vine, you are the branches. He who abides in Me, and I in him, bears much fruit. By this My Father is glorified, that you bear much fruit."

JOHN 15:1–2, 5, 8

Notice that your Father has a plan—the biggest, most beautiful harvest possible.

Notice telltale signs of His utter dedication—not one branch is overlooked.

Feel the singular passion that He pours into His special object of affection—the branches.

From Him will come the power and provision to accomplish His Father's work.

In this chapter we'll look more closely at the picture of the vineyard Jesus described. Because every word He said is really about you—your life today, your relationship with God, and your amazing future.

YOUR LIFE AS A BRANCH

Three distinct persons are represented in the picture that Jesus gave that night in the vineyard.

1. *Jesus is the vine* (v. 1). In a vineyard, the vine is the main stem or trunk that grows up out of the ground. Interestingly, the vine doesn't produce the fruit—the branches do that.

   Jesus is telling His disciples that He is their source of life. From Him will come the power and provision to accomplish His Father's work on earth.

2. *God the Father is the Vinedresser* (v. 1). A vinedresser is the owner or tender of the vineyard. He cares for each branch in such a way that it produces the most grapes possible.

   Since the role of a grower is so much like that of a parent, it shouldn't surprise us that Jesus identified God the Father as the Vinedresser.

3. *Every follower of Christ is a branch* (v. 5). In a vineyard, several branches grow from each vine. They are tied to stakes or wires for support and care. Every new shoot, leaf, or tendril is carefully tended with the

harvest to come in mind. And what the vinedresser has in mind is fruit.

Are you a follower of Christ? Then you're a branch. For your whole life, God has been purposefully at work on your branch like a passionate, attentive vinedresser. Every intervention in your life circumstances has been with a goal in mind. And what a goal it is—a great harvest for God's glory!

For too many years, bearing fruit as a Christian was a vague concept to me.

You can tell Jesus didn't want His disciples to miss the point because He summarized the meaning of His vineyard picture again in verse 16:

> *"You did not choose Me, but I chose you and appointed you that you should go and bear fruit, and that your fruit should remain."*

Jesus was leaving them—and us!—with a very important assignment. He wants us to bear spiritual fruit that will last forever.

But what exactly is fruit?

A Passion for More

After she read *Secrets of the Vine,* a woman named Sarena sent Bruce a note. "I don't have another day to waste," she said. "I've wasted too many years already. I want to be a passionate Christian. I want my life to be an overflowing basket for God."

I understand Sarena's urgency about doing something significant with her life. But I have to admit that for too many years, bearing fruit as a Christian was a vague concept to me. I thought it was something pastors and evangelists did mostly from the platform in front of large crowds. And I was absolutely terrified of speaking in public!

If I could hand you a piece of paper and ask you to list one "fruit" that was part of your life yesterday, what would you write down?

If you are giving this page a blank stare, perhaps it's because you are uncertain, as I was for so long, as to how to understand fruit in a woman's life. You may be as eager as Sarena to bear fruit for God, yet you may have no idea what that activity actually looks like.

Let's look at the New Testament for help. In the following three verses, one word occurs repeatedly in association with the idea of spiritual fruitfulness.

Ephesians 5:11—"Have no fellowship with the *unfruitful works* of darkness."

Colossians 1:10—"Walk worthy of the Lord, fully pleasing Him, being *fruitful* in *every good work.*"

Titus 3:14—"And let our people also learn to maintain *good works,* to meet urgent needs, that they may not be *unfruitful.*"

I'm sure it's plain to you now. A fruit for God is a good work for Him—something you do that helps someone else and brings God glory.

Now if I ask you to list a good work you've done recently, your pen should flow more easily. Or maybe you're like me and what comes to mind first is a work for God with someone else's name and face on it . . .

CREATED FOR THIS

I think of Jan, for instance. Her seventy-year old mother-in-law fell last week and broke her leg in two places. Even with three active teenagers, Jan is patiently and joyfully doing everything she can to nurse her mother-in-law back to health.

I think, too, of Jennifer, a full-time office worker. Somebody once described her work environment as the "Snake Pit." Yet everyone notices her positive attitude and patience with others (including a demanding boss). And they know their clients count on Jennifer because of her integrity under pressure.

And Regina, mother of four small boys. Her husband is on the road a lot, but she works hard to make coming home the best part of his week, including having the children ready and waiting at the door with hugs for Daddy.

And Teri, a breath of encouragement. She is confined to a wheelchair because of a car accident. She spends a lot of time each week praying for the needs in her local congregation. When friends visit, they usually leave saying the same thing: "I went to encourage Teri and left encouraged myself."

What a great question to ask yourself: Have I done what I could?

Too many women I know think of singing in the choir or teaching a Sunday school class as the *real* good works, and the ordinary tasks of serving others throughout the day as somehow less significant. Even the disciples had that problem.

Imagine how Mary must have felt when they criticized her for anointing Jesus' head with her vial of perfume (Mark 14:3–9). The Bible says they were indignant and "criticized her sharply" (v. 5). Ouch!

You see, the disciples thought the oil would have had a more spiritual use if it had been sold and the money given to charity. But Jesus stepped in to the argument. "Let her alone," He said. "She has done a good work for Me" (v. 6).

So we need to change our mind about the good works ready and waiting for each of us to offer up to God. Our opportunities don't very often require a platform, or an extraordinary talent, or an unusual opportunity. They require a heart that is ready to do a good work for Jesus at a moment's notice.

Perhaps the reason the Bible doesn't record all possible good works is that there are too many to list! Yet what the Bible does say about good works is even more amazing. I'm thinking about Paul's statement in Ephesians 2:

> *For we are His workmanship, created in Christ Jesus for good works, which God prepared beforehand that we should walk in them.*
>
> V. 10

What an incredible thought! You and I have been created for the purpose of doing good works. God designed you, He gifted you, and He placed you in the world so that the fruit of your life would have an everlasting impact. He even prepared those activities for you before you were born.

Out of all the centuries in time, this is the generation into which God chose to place you. Of course, you had nothing to do with the country in which you were born or the family you were born into. But clearly God placed you in His world at this particular time so that you could do something special.

Now I want you to notice what Jesus went on to say about Mary's simple act of selflessness: "She has done what she could" (Mark 14:8). What a great question to ask yourself at the end of a day! *Have I done what I could?*

I encourage you to ask God to show you every day what your specially prepared works are, and to help you do them for His glory. Once a woman sees the eternity-plan of the Vinedresser surfacing in every ordinary day, it's hard to go back to that boring old life you used to walk through.

Let me give you a personal example.

Walking in Good Works

I remember thinking about Ephesians 2:10 one day when suddenly the words *that we should walk in them* leaped out at me. Walk in good works? What was I to make of that?

At the time, we lived in a small blue house where I spent my days caring for the needs of two small children and a busy husband. Bruce was beginning to travel more and more as the Lord blessed his teaching ministry, Walk Thru the Bible. For me, on the other hand, "travel" usually meant a dash to the grocery store or doctor's office, and then it was back to the little blue house. My purse, my wardrobe, and most of my dreams smelled of graham crackers.

Can you relate?

One morning I heard a knock at the door. A young mom from down the street was standing there in tears. When I invited her in, she told me that her three misbehaving children had pushed her to the end of her rope. She needed help, but didn't know where to turn.

I can still picture us sitting together drinking hot tea at the kitchen table. Since I had recently been reading in Proverbs during my quiet time, it felt natural to show her several verses that gave wisdom about family discipline. She left an hour or so later, encouraged and committed to dealing with her children by using God's principles.

That was the day I understood what the Bible meant by walking in good works. I was busy doing the works at home that God had called me to do for that season of my life. To my Lord, they were beautiful, and honoring, and enough. When the time was right, God didn't suddenly drop me into an auditorium or an international travel schedule. He brought me another mother in tears about her children. She was standing right in front of me, on the porch of my little blue house.

Picture yourself getting up in the morning and walking through your day. (You may feel like sprinting or running through your day is a little more realistic!) Look over your list of tasks and routines and people who depend on you. Every activity represents a good work for you to walk in— a work that is yours to do, and yours to give the Lord. You just have to be ready to see it, and ready to do it with your whole heart.

I think it's interesting that Jesus said to "go and *bear* fruit," not to "go and *find* fruit." When you think about it, bringing life into the world is something women have understood since Eve ("be fruitful and multiply"). And it is our privilege and honor, no matter where we are, to bear spiritual fruit for Him. And a lot of it!

Jesus said, "By this my Father is glorified, that you bear *much fruit*" (John 15:8).

BASKETS OF ABUNDANCE

Think about it: It's not our good intentions to be fruitful that bring our Father glory. It's not even how hard we try. It is how much fruit comes from our branch. Each branch bears a different amount of fruit, and all fruit honors God. But God's greatest glory comes from the ones who bear much fruit.

If you look closely at Jesus' teaching in John 15, you'll notice four levels of fruit bearing:

Level 1—no fruit ("every branch in Me that *does not bear fruit,*" v. 2, emphasis added).

Level 2—fruit ("every branch that bears *fruit,*" v. 2).

Level 3—more fruit ("that it may bear *more fruit,*" v. 2).

Level 4—much fruit ("bears *much fruit,*" vv. 5, 8).

Where do you think your level of fruit bearing is at this very moment? If the Master Vinedresser harvested your branch this year for His glory, how much honor would He receive? A lot? Some? A little? None?

If you sense that you are among those branches that could bear a lot more fruit, be encouraged! God cares so much about the outcome of your fruitfulness that you can count on Him to work continuously in your life toward a huge harvest for Him.

In the chapters to come, we're going to learn what God does to take us from one level of fruitfulness to the next, and then to the next. We'll call His methods "secrets," but really they are very simple truths that every believer can understand. Once you know them, I think you'll agree that a life of overflowing spiritual abundance is God's dream for every one of His children.

For whom the L<small>ORD</small> loves
He corrects, just as a father the son
in whom he delights.

P<small>ROVERBS</small> 3:12

CHAPTER THREE

Lifted by Love

During the night, the sound of distant thunder awoke the young woman. She lay in bed, listening to a scattering of raindrops on the leaves outside her window. It was not good news. Only two days remained before the harvest, and the weather was not cooperating.

Outside, lightning flashed. The young woman knew her father was awake and concerned, too.

She still remembered the first time a severe storm hit the vineyard. She'd followed her father on his rounds as he carried a bucket of water. "Look at this branch," he said, pointing to one that was half buried in mud. She watched as he knelt down and set to work. He gently washed the branch off and tied it up to the trellis again.

"What are you doing?" she asked.

"Helping this branch get better," he said.

"Is it sick?"

"Yes, you could say that."

"Does it have a temperature, Papa?"

"No. It fell into the dirt in a storm."

"Doesn't it want to grow any more grapes?"

"Of course it does! In fact, someday it will grow more grapes than you could eat in a week!"

Now as the young woman listened to the plinking of the rain, she thought about how gentle and caring her father had been to each branch as he went about his work.

And with that thought, she drifted back to sleep.

It didn't seem like such a terrible thing. At least, not while I was in the department store on my lunch break. The cashier had misread the price tag and undercharged me several dollars. I recall thinking, "What a blessing! I got a real discount!" At the time, Bruce was a seminary student and I was working full-time to help pay the bills. *The Lord must be providing a little extra through her mistake,* I decided.

But as I walked out the door, an uninvited question burst into my thoughts: *What's the biblical term for what you just did?*

The answer flashed through my mind: *stealing.*

I wish I could tell you that I turned around and made things right, but I didn't. Actually, I decided that the store had lots of money, and Bruce and I didn't, and I put it out of my mind.

Lifted by Love

But when I crawled into bed that night, my unexpected "blessing" kept coming to mind, and I tossed and turned for hours. In the morning, I dashed off to work promising myself to return the money on my lunch hour.

At noon, halfway through my sandwich, I reached for my pocket New Testament. Opening it at random, I read James 4:17: "Therefore, to him who knows to do good and does not do it, to him it is sin." (So much for random reading!)

But I still didn't go back to that store.

Instead, I returned to work only to go home early because of a terrible headache. By now, I felt both physically and spiritually ill. And angry, too. *This is ridiculous,* I fumed. *It's only a few dollars! Why should I torture and humiliate myself over so little?*

But as I lay on my bed, I saw that it was not a little thing. In fact, those few stolen dollars were really just the latest symptom of a growing and very unattractive pattern in my life. I saw attitudes of rebellion, resistance, and compromise that I had been excusing for too long. No wonder I'd been feeling so spiritually unmotivated.

> *Those few stolen dollars were a symptom of a very unattractive pattern in my life.*

Has God ever seemed to ambush you with the truth like that?

This chapter is about how our Father intervenes to rescue us from the mud of our own wrong choices. Jesus' teachings in the vineyard show us that unaddressed sin in our lives is like dirt on the grape branch of our lives. It cuts out the air and sun, and makes fruit bearing nearly impossible. We need help!

The good news is that our Father the Vinedresser has a plan for our future. And the plan is as wonderful as it is surprising.

LIFTED BY LOVE

In His vineyard teaching, Jesus spoke very directly about what God does with the branch that is barren:

> *"Every branch in Me that does not bear fruit*
> *He takes away."*
>
> v. 2

Since Jesus identified every branch "in Me," we know He was speaking only about believers. The New Testament often describes the believer as a person who is "in Christ" (for examples, see Ephesians 2:10 and Philippians 3:9).

But "takes away"? That doesn't sound very promising, does it?

Some have taught that God literally discards an unfruitful Christian. But a closer look at the meaning of the Greek word *airo*—here translated as "takes away" or "cuts off"—shows a much different and more hopeful picture.

If you've read *Secrets of the Vine*, you remember how Bruce's study of the original language, along with a chance conversation with a grape grower, turned on the lights for him on this passage. A stronger rendering of *airo* is "lift up" or "take up." (Other New Testament passages support this reading of *airo*. The same word is used, for example, when the disciples took up twelve baskets of food after the feeding of the five thousand in Matthew 14:20, and when Simon was forced to carry Christ's cross in Matthew 27:32.)

> *God loves us too much not to intervene when we slide off course.*

And according to the California vineyard keeper, "lift up" is exactly what growers do to grape branches that are trailing in the dirt. The branch is too valuable to cut off and throw away. Instead, the vinedresser carefully lifts the dirty branches, washes them off, and ties them up in the sun so they can begin producing again.

You and I are too valuable to be discarded by our Father, too. Instead of throwing us away, He will step in to bring us back to fruitfulness. But what does this process look like in our lives?

That's the wonderful news of the first secret of the vine.

> **FIRST SECRET OF THE VINE:**
>
> *If your life consistently bears no fruit,*
> *God will intervene to discipline you*
> *so you will bear fruit.*

The truth is that God loves us too much not to intervene when we slide off course. He pursues us and disciplines us through our whole lives because He still has a plan for our best. And that best, says Jesus, looks a lot like a branch full of beautiful grapes.

TRAINING DAYS

Wouldn't it be great if we could just experience God's best in life without a little redirection? Then again, wouldn't it be great if our kids would do the right thing without ever needing a reminder from us? Or maybe several reminders? Or maybe losing a coveted privilege? Ouch!

You see how easy it is to go from the need to bring correction to the subject of...pain?!

Scripture uses words parents are familiar with, like *discipline* and *chastening*, to describe how God redirects His children. For example, these verses in Hebrews:

> If you endure chastening, God deals with you as with sons; for what son is there whom a father does not chasten? But if you are without chastening, of which all have become partakers, then you are illegitimate and not sons.
>
> HEBREWS 12:7–8

We'd like to think that God the Father would choose a disciplinary response that got wonderful results without pain. But not so. Hebrews assures us of that:

> *Now no chastening seems to be joyful for the present, but painful; nevertheless, afterward it yields the peaceable fruit of righteousness to those who have been trained by it.*
>
> V. 11

If you're like me, you have a strong dislike for pain. I am

on "red alert" the moment I feel it. But the truth is, years ago I used the same "red alert" response to teach my young children. First a warning: "Jessica, honey! Don't touch the stove! It's hot!" If that didn't work, a smack on her little hand came next: "Jessica, listen and obey! I said don't touch the stove! You'll burn yourself!"

You understand what I'm saying, don't you? The pain of that smack on your child's hand has only one purpose—you sincerely want to prevent her from experiencing a much greater pain. The goal of your discipline is that your child will "be trained by it."

We should never think that all suffering comes from God.

Of course, God doesn't physically smack our straying hands. Instead, He works through people and circumstances to train up His children. If we respond positively to the pain, we turn more and more in His direction. And the result is the "peaceable fruit of righteousness."

We should never think that all suffering comes from God. God is the source of every good and perfect gift (James 1:17). But we happen to live in a fallen world where disease, evil people, and natural disasters can strike at any time. God understands our pain so deeply that He chose to send His own Son to bring us redemption and eternal life. Yet the Bible makes it clear that God will use discomfort or suffering in our lives to get our attention, to turn us away from harm, and to turn us toward abundance.

Does our Father *want* to cause us discomfort or anguish? Of course not.

Will our Father stop pursuing us with His best? Not even when we break His heart.

And not even if we don't pay attention the first time.

"Whom the Lord Loves"

As every mom knows, there's a big difference in how you discipline Johnny if he spends his Sunday school offering on candy once, and how you discipline him if he is stealing grievously and repeatedly. In the same way, God's discipline is always in proportion to the seriousness of the sin. Jesus taught the principle of escalating discipline in Matthew 18:15–17, and we see it repeated in Hebrews.

Notice the underlined words in the following verses. They show three different labels for discipline, suggesting increasing degrees of intensity:

And you have forgotten the exhortation which speaks to you as to sons:

> *"My son, do not despise the chastening of the LORD,
> nor be discouraged when you are <u>rebuked</u> by Him;
> For whom the LORD loves He <u>chastens</u>, and <u>scourges</u>
> every son whom He receives."*
>
> HEBREWS 12:5-6

A rebuke is a spoken warning. If you think about it, you'll agree that in an average day, 99 percent of a young mother's discipline comes through words of rebuke. We may receive rebukes from a friend, a pastor, a word of Scripture, or directly from the Holy Spirit.

Discipline is a family word that proves our Father's love and assures us that we are His children.

Chastening seems to show a more serious level of discipline (verse 11 in the same chapter describes it as "painful"). I've experienced this level of discipline as emotional anxiety, distress, or an ongoing circumstance of extreme frustration.

The third level, scourging, points to physical pain. Scourging is what the Roman soldiers did to Jesus with whips. Spiritually, this level of discipline is probably reserved for Christians who are living in open sin, having lost any concern for what God wants or how their actions are affecting others.

You and I can trust that God's ways with us are always wise and good, and with one goal in mind. The psalmist wrote, "Before I was afflicted I went astray, but now I keep Your word" (Psalm 119:67). God's goal is always our obedience to His will, because in His will is our best.

Sadly, Christians you and I know are suffering every day unnecessarily because they have not heard or acted on the truth of God's discipline. They misinterpret unwanted circumstances and emotions as random events when they are actually God's efforts to set them free from sin and bring them back to fruitfulness.

> *God's discipline is always in proportion to the seriousness of the sin.*

Some of us even act on the lie that we can hang onto ongoing sin, bear fruit for God . . . and experience no other unwanted consequences. As a result, we experience unnecessary suffering and a broken relationship with our heavenly Father.

But it doesn't have to be that way. Just ask some women who have been there . . .

Don't Mix These Words Up

Be sure not to confuse God's discipline with punishment. Discipline is for God's children; punishment is for His enemies. Punishment includes anger, wrath, and the intent to make someone pay for their offenses. When Christ hung on the cross over two thousand years ago, He took on Himself the punishment we deserved for our sins. He "bore our sins in His own body on the tree, that we, having died to sins, might live for righteousness" (1 Peter 2:24). The moment we believe by faith that through His death and resurrection Jesus paid the full penalty for our sins, the word punishment ceases to apply to us.

However, even though our sins are forgiven, their consequences will bring harm to us, to others, and to our relationship with God. That's why His loving correction is so important. *Discipline* is a family word that proves our Father's love and assures us that we are His children.

In Him we have redemption through His blood, the forgiveness of sins, according to the riches of His grace.

EPHESIANS 1:7

STORIES ON THE ROAD TO BOUNTIFUL

"I'd been feeling unexplainable frustration and anger even though things were going well," wrote Nicole, after reading *Secrets of the Vine*. "I couldn't figure out what was causing the feelings until one night when I sat down to write in my journal. After a two-page prayer, I saw it clearly. I had been unable to forgive myself and others for some things that had happened, and so I assumed that God wasn't able to forgive me either."

As Nicole poured out her tears and her confession to God, He began to bring back the relief that had been missing. She says she feels a new sense of peace now. "Just doing the dishes feels more restful. It is so good to be personal with God again."

Then there's Amy, a single mom who came to the Lord about a year ago when a Christian drama group visited her Atlanta neighborhood. She left behind a life of drug and alcohol addiction. She went back to school to earn her GED. She took many brave steps toward a God-honoring life. But she continued to have a sexual relationship with her boyfriend.

> *She took brave steps toward a God-honoring life. But she continued to have a sexual relationship with her boyfriend.*

God didn't deal with Amy on this issue the moment she became saved. Instead, He allowed her time to grow and to understand His ways and His will for her life. "Then came a gentle rebuke in the form of a friend's concern," she says. "And when I went for counseling, the pastor was even more frank with me about what God requires of His children in the way of sexual purity."

You may be one choice away, as I was, from a fresh start with God.

But still, Amy didn't want to change this part of her life. "I was afraid of losing my boyfriend and he didn't want to marry me." The pressure on Amy's life increased when she wanted to work with the junior high group at church. She knew she couldn't do so until she resolved this issue.

"Then things got even tougher for me," she admits. "My boyfriend betrayed me with another woman. I lost my job at the library. I felt like my whole life was falling apart. And that did it. I repented—and probably just in time." Since then, Amy has been finding many ministry opportunities helping other young women who are struggling with the same issues.

At a recent conference I attended, a woman gave this incredible testimony. In her case, she had allowed God's discipline to progress to a much more intense level:

"Six months ago I was diagnosed with an incurable disease and told to get my affairs in order. I went to my pastor, who wisely asked, 'Are there any regrets in your life?' After some reflection, I told him I'd held a deep grudge against my sister for more than ten years, even though my bitterness had harmed myself and others. 'Are you willing to forgive her now?' asked the pastor. When I said yes, he led me through a time of confession and repentance for my anger, hurtfulness and bitterness. Then I went to my sister and asked if we could talk about our broken relationship. I confessed my grudge, and told her I knew that my bitterness toward her was sin. Then I begged for her forgiveness. She did forgive me, and we shared a very meaningful time together. I left feeling cleansed and free to love her again. Within weeks, my symptoms unexpectedly disappeared. In fact, the doctors can find no trace of the disease. That's why I now firmly believe that ongoing sin in a Christian's life has both spiritual and physical consequences."

Your story may not be as dramatic as these. Or it may be

> *That experience showed me the source of my spiritual barrenness, and it revealed to me God's ongoing desire for my restoration.*

much more dramatic! God has such an amazing adventure ahead for each of us. Whatever your circumstances right now, I imagine that if you looked back over your own life, you could identify a time when serious, unaddressed sin cut you off from God's blessings and put you directly in the path of His discipline.

I walked up to a very surprised store manager and handed him his dollars along with my apology.

Don't let God's precious investment in you go to waste! Ask, *What did I learn in those times? What do I now know about God that I didn't before? How have I changed for the better?*

You might decide you are experiencing your Father's discipline right now. If so, I encourage you to carefully evaluate your beliefs and actions. You may be one choice away, as I was, from a fresh start with God.

The Waters of Repentance

Looking back on my department store misadventure, I'm almost glad I didn't immediately return those few dollars. Why? Because that experience showed me the source of my spiritual barrenness, and it revealed to me God's ongoing desire for my restoration.

Old Obstacles, New Breakthrough Beliefs

adapted from *Secrets of the Vine Bible Study*

We never have to be enslaved by sin, repeating the same destructive patterns (Romans 6:11–12). But at times, our human thinking can hold us hostage to lies. Choose the false beliefs that most seem to be keeping you from making a change today. Let the Bible help you discover a new breakthrough truth, and write it down (in your own words) in your journal.

1. The "I Can Outlast God" Strategy. *You believe that God will eventually give up and leave you alone.* Psalm 139:7–12; Luke 15:1–7.

2. The "If You Can't Beat 'Em, Join 'Em" Defense. *You believe that you can't give up your sin. You've tried many times; why try again?* Romans 6:14; 1 Corinthians 10:1–13; 2 Peter 2:9.

3. The "Big, Mean God" Assumption. *You believe that God is wrong to cause you pain no matter what you've done.* Job 5:17–18; Psalm 145:8–9; Ezekiel 33:11; Hebrews 12:5–17.

4. The "Ostrich" Maneuver. *You think that if you don't think God will intervene, He probably won't.* Galatians 6:7–10; Philippians 2:12–13.

5. The "No Fire Now Means No Fire Later" Gamble. *You believe that if God doesn't discipline you immediately when you sin, He won't do anything later, either.* Romans 2:4–11; 1 Corinthians 11:31–32; 2 Peter 3:1–9.

Lying on my bed that afternoon, I finally submitted to His discipline. In tearful repentance, I confessed my sin, not only of stealing but also of stubbornly-held attitudes of rebellion and compromise. I recommitted myself to doing the right thing, no matter what the cost. The next morning, I walked up to a very surprised store manager, handed him his dollars along with my apology, and walked out of there a very relieved and renewed woman!

> *You are drenched with peace when you say yes to your Father, the Vinedresser!*

Imagine yourself standing in a cool, clear forest pool. Your arms are open wide. Your face is up. Your eyes are closed. A pure, cool waterfall is splashing over you and around you . . . and you are drenched with peace.

That's how it feels when you say yes to your Father, the Vinedresser, as He washes away the sin that's covering your life!

I invite you right now to quiet your heart before the Lord. Ask Him if there is anything in your life that is grieving Him. Then be still before Him for the next sixty seconds.

It might be the longest minute you've experienced in a long time, but if you say yes to whatever God is asking you to do, it will be the best sixty seconds, too!

Now let's return to the vineyard and discover God's surprising plan to prepare you and me—not just to have *some* spiritual fruit in our lives, but *more* fruit.

Much more!

*"Every branch that
bears fruit He prunes, that it
may bear more fruit."*

JOHN 15:2

CHAPTER FOUR

Making Room for More

The truckloads of baskets arrived before dawn. The woman and her father were out early to make sure that baskets were deposited at each row, ready for the pickers to begin the day's work.

This was the first day of harvest: the day that the calendar of vineyard life rushed toward, the day when the results of work done months before would become apparent for everyone to see. Fortunately, the weather had turned mild and dry—perfect for protecting the ripe fruit from damage or mold.

The hours passed in a flurry of picking, carrying overflowing baskets to the truck, and driving the loads of harvested grapes to town. For the next several weeks, the busy scene in the vineyard would be repeated until the last grape was picked.

Late in the afternoon, when the pickers had gone home, the young woman sat in the shade of an arbor with her father. Their hands were stained, their backs were tired—and they were both elated. Every sign pointed to an exceptional year.

"Papa," she began, "even the older men were remarking today about your grapes. They can't remember picking such stunning fruit. I heard them shouting 'Bellisimo! Bellisimo!' all over the vineyard!"

"Umm," he responded contentedly, his eyes half-closed.

"They say all of Tuscany will remember this harvest," she continued. "When I went with the trucks to town today, everyone there wanted to know your secret."

"And what did you tell them?"

"I told them what you always say." She turned playfully to face him, then recited, "The secret of taking more to town in September is leaving more behind all year long."

"What an excellent student you are, my dear!" he exclaimed. "But did they understand?"

"Some," she mused. "But not many."

The vinedresser in our story understood and applied the wonderful principle of "leaving more behind." If you're a home gardener, I imagine you do, too. Early every spring you pay special attention to your dwarf apple trees or your prize rose bushes. Why? Because you know that the size and condition of the fruit or flowers you hope to enjoy later in the year will depend on what you do now.

And what you have to do now is prune.

One gardening manual in our house defines pruning as "removing unwanted plant parts for a purpose." You cut away unnecessary shoots. You pinch back buds and foliage to redirect growth. Your purpose is more fruit or bigger blooms.

The same is true in our spiritual lives. Jesus shared a second powerful secret of the vine that night in the vineyard when He said, "Every branch that bears fruit He prunes, that it may bear more fruit" (v. 2).

> *Pruning is God's way of making room in your life for more of what matters most.*

Clearly, Jesus wanted you and me to understand what God, in His great love for us, does to increase our fruitfulness.

The whole idea of spiritual pruning tells us that we have to let go of a lot of our "pretty good" to receive God's very best. This surprising truth is at the heart of the second secret of the vine.

> ## SECOND SECRET OF THE VINE:
> *If your life bears some fruit,*
> *God will intervene to prune you...*
> *so that you will bear more fruit.*

In a grape plant, pruning redirects the sap away from wasteful growth and toward desirable fruit. In our lives, pruning is God's way of making room for more of what matters most, and redirecting the flow of His life through us so that we'll produce more of what will last for eternity.

Even though being pruned isn't much fun, the purpose for it is full of promise. In fact, if you cooperate with God's shears, you'll soon find yourself shaking your head—not over what you have left behind, but at the wonderful new results you see flourishing all around.

THE TROUBLE WITH LEAVES

Think of leaves as those activities, preoccupations, and priorities that, though not wrong, are using up valuable resources that would be better spent in pursuit of fruitfulness for God.

I don't know about you, but I'm especially skilled at producing an abundance of "leaves" in my life! As women, we enjoy creating an attractive, comfortable life for those we love. But we can get so caught up in the demands of the immediate that we leave no room for the future God is trying to give us.

For my friend Gail, teaching a weekly Bible study in her home had for years been a fulfilling and fruitful activity. For some time, though, busyness had kept her from taking the next step—one that was wide open to her—of developing a video teaching curriculum that would reach many more with the same material. Last year she finally took a step of faith. She reprioritized her activities, turned her group over to a woman she had been mentoring, and headed for the recording studio.

> *She had been busy doing good. But God was inviting her to reach for His best.*

"I always prayed that God would use me to teach more women," she told me, "but I wanted to do it my way. Giving up certain activities was difficult. But already God is using the video teaching to reach thousands of women I could never touch personally."

As God begins to prune in your life, your first reaction may be to wail, "What have I done wrong?" But the truth is that if God is pruning you, you're doing something right!

You're not bogged down in ongoing, serious sin. You're already busy bearing fruit. But your loving Father wants to help you bear "more fruit" for His glory.

Was Gail doing something wrong? Of course not. She had been busy doing good. But God was inviting her to do more—to reach for His best.

God doesn't prune away sin—that's what He does with His discipline. His pruning focuses on the second-

Discipline Versus Pruning: A Comparison

Issue	Disciplining	Pruning
How do you know it's happening?	Pain	Discomfort
Why is it happening?	You're doing something wrong (sin)	You're doing something right (bearing fruit)
What is your level of fruitfulness?	No fruit	Fruit
What is the Vinedresser's desire?	Fruit	More fruit
What needs to go?	Sin (disobeying the Lord)	Self (putting myself before God)
How should you feel?	Guilty, sad	Relief, trust
What is the right response?	Repentance (stop your sin)	Release (surrender to God)
When does it stop?	When you stop your sin	When God is finished

best pursuits that can take over our lives, or on values or activities that used to be a priority for us but shouldn't be any longer. They can waste our potential for weeks or months. Maybe even for a lifetime.

What God's Shears Look Like

Of course, God doesn't come marching into your kitchen brandishing an enormous pair of pruning shears! So how does He work?

As we'll see, God prunes people indirectly. He works through His people and our key relationships. He speaks to us through His Word. He nudges us through the press of challenging circumstances—perhaps trials at home, on the job, or in our finances. He leads by the insistent voice of His Spirit in our hearts.

However God chooses to work, He will get our attention, creating discomfort if necessary, so that we can focus on and respond to the point of His pruning.

Since every branch in Christ gets pruned, we know that the Vinedresser is at work everywhere in the family of God right now—including your life and mine! Having spent years talking to women on this subject, I've noticed a recurring pattern of focal points for God's pruning shears:

- Priorities that need to be rearranged
- Relationships that need to change or end
- Busyness that isn't accomplishing what matters most
- Dependencies or attachments that we're ready to grow out of
- Personal "rights" that God is asking us to surrender to Him

Where do you think God might be pruning in your life today?

If you have no idea, try this: Look for recurring pressure points (you could call them "invitations") in your reading of God's Word, your conversations with your spiritual mentors, the challenges you've faced recently. Tell God you're ready to acknowledge His will and surrender with an open heart.

SHEAR AMAZEMENT: STORIES OF LIFE AFTER PRUNING

George Mueller wrote, "Our Father never takes anything from his children unless he means to give them something better." Do you believe that? I do! And so do the women you're about to meet. They have responded to the Vinedresser's pruning, too, and discovered God's "something better."

Donna: "Fixing Brad was not my personal responsibility."

Donna admits she was constantly trying to get her husband, Brad, to read his Bible and be more spiritual. One day, Brad picked up the latest Christian book she had handed him and threw it across the room. "If you don't stop nagging me," he announced angrily, "I'll walk out that door and never come back!" Frightened and heartsick, Donna asked God what to do.

"The following months were intensely painful as God went to work in my heart," she recalls. A friend helped her see that it was not her job to make Brad holy. "I realized that my worry and well-intentioned meddling were getting in God's way," she says. When she let God change her attitudes and actions, things changed with Brad, too. Says Donna, "There is more harmony in our marriage and more spiritual openness today than I ever could have accomplished my way."

"I was able to share my heart with these women because I knew how it felt to have nothing."

Janis: "Our home and all our possessions are always on loan."

Janis and her husband had been married for twenty-five years when through an act of arson their home burned to the ground. "Everything we owned was gone," she says. "It took only days, through the kindness of friends and family, to begin a new home, but it took months for me to let go emotionally of all I had lost. I wept every time I remembered a baby photo album or a gift from one of my children."

Eventually, Janis saw that even though the Lord mourned her loss with her, He was inviting her to grow from it. She volunteered for a program at her church to help homeless women. "I was able to genuinely share my heart with these women because I knew how it felt to have nothing. I came to realize that God used this tragedy as a surprise opportunity for pruning."

With him gone, she spent most evenings idly watching television or brooding.

Today, Janis and her husband serve as missionaries. She says, "Without learning that my possessions are on loan from God, I could never have left everything to serve Him overseas. But what we're seeing now is fruit that will last forever. And we've never been happier!"

Margie: "My illness was not a mistake."

Tall, striking, and outgoing, Margie was a born leader who was busy using her gifts for God. But one day, Margie became ill and had to be hospitalized. After an operation, the surgeon announced that she would have to feed herself through a tube inserted into her stomach for the rest of her life.

"Month after month I sought the Lord for healing to be able to return to my work for Him," she recalls. For three years, Margie suffered with her debilitating condition, and then one day God miraculously healed her. The stomach tube was removed, she regained her strength, and gradually she began to minister again. But Margie was an amazingly different person. In fact, her work with others has been dramatically more effective because of her increased sensitivity and compassion.

> *For years God has been asking for me to surrender my expectations to Him.*

"I learned that while God has plans for our gifts and abilities, He can have even greater plans for our desperate need of Him," she says now. "I believe God pruned me through my illness so that I could relate better to the daily struggles of others. That's where real ministry begins anyway."

Mavis: *"I let God peel my fingers off my husband's job."*

Mavis had been praying for years that God would bring her husband Ed a job that would allow him to be at home every evening. With him gone, she spent most evenings idly watching television or brooding.

"I was miserable until I let God peel my fingers off what I wanted and accepted the opportunities He had been trying to give me—time with my kids, time to encourage single moms we know, time to seek Him," she says. "The quality of our family life has changed completely."

Mavis is still praying for a different job for Ed. But she has taken a huge step forward in maturity and impact for God.

Sandy: "My perfect voice was not the voice others could hear best."

A gifted young singer, Sandy loved serving the Lord with her voice. Then she developed a lump in her throat. When surgery left her with damaged vocal cords, Sandy was devastated. She couldn't understand why her greatest gift had been taken from her.

For two years, Sandy continued to write songs but refused to sing. One Sunday, as a favor to her husband, she sang his favorite song during the evening service. A visitor, who happened to be the president of a recording company, was so moved by the emotional power of her singing that he offered Sandy a contract. Her CD is now being distributed through a mission organization to churches around the world.

"God took away my 'perfect' voice," Sandy says, "and gave me a voice that would reach more people in deeper ways for Him."

Nora: *"I decided to give up my 'right' to be married."*

Ever since she had become a believer, Nora felt she had a "right" to be married. In the past, this attitude had led her into destructive relationships with non-Christian men. Even though she had put an end to those, Nora still held tightly to her belief that God owed her a husband.

"As I learned about the principle of pruning, I saw that for years God has been asking for me to surrender my expectations to Him," she says. One night she tearfully relinquished a long list of "rights"—to be married, to be in control, to be thin. "Most of all," she says, "my 'right' to continually mourn the mistakes I have made in the past."

> *Pruning always involves surrender and relinquishment on our part.*

"I can't describe the peace I now have," Nora says. "When anxiety begins to arise over 'What do I do now?' I simply give the Lord my 'right' to worry. These days, I'm enjoying much healthier relationships with others, and the blessed assurance that the Lord has always known what is best for me. Of course, being the perfect gentleman that He is, He has never forced His best on me!"

With Open Hands

As you've listened to these women's stories, what has the Lord brought to your mind? You might have realized that in your life, the Vinedresser has been pruning you in an important area that is unique to you. He may be asking you to say yes to His hand in your finances, your desire to be comfortable or secure, a family situation, or a new season of your life.

I didn't understand that every gift in this life has a time limit.

Pruning always involves surrender and relinquishment on our part. God asks us to keep our hands open to His ways and His will. He may ask us to let go of something that feels important to our happiness. No wonder we feel discomfort or even pain in pruning! Yet we know from James 1:17 that "every good gift and every perfect gift is from above, and comes down from the Father." So my encouragement to you is to receive His pruning as nothing less than an unexpected, unasked-for, but exceedingly precious gift! Because that's what pruning is. As, George McDonald wrote, "God's fingers can touch nothing except to mold it into loveliness."

Making Room for More

Here's something I've learned about God's gifts that has meant a great deal to me:

I grew up believing that everything I love, treasure, enjoy, and consider good on earth is a gift from God. But I didn't understand that every gift in this life has a time limit. People die, possessions can be destroyed, and positions taken away. That's just the way life is. And if I assume that everything I hold in my hand today is mine to keep, I will be deeply disappointed. Ultimately, I'll begin to question God's character and His intentions toward me—and that can spell big trouble.

So besides keeping my hands open, I've imagined a place for an expiration date written on the back of each treasure in my life. Then I leave it up to God to fill in that date. Why not? He is the only one who knows my future anyway. And He is the only one who knows what would be best for me. As David wrote:

> *But as for me, I trust in You, O LORD;*
> *I say, "You are my God."*
> *My times are in Your hand.*
>
> PSALM 31:14–15

Pruning means we lose something now to gain something later.

Cutting Loose from Pruning Tangles
adapted from *Secrets of the Vine Bible Study*

If you recognize yourself in any of the false beliefs below, let God's Word prepare you to receive the work of abundance He wants for your life. Then write out your new breakthrough belief in your journal.

1. You think, "God is picking on me unfairly." 2 Corinthians 1:3–7; Hebrews 5:8–9; James 1:2–12; 1 Peter 1:6–7.

2. You assume, "God has abandoned me." Psalm 23; Psalm 139:1–6; Daniel 3:15–18; John 14:18; Romans 8:35–39.

3. You exclaim, "God is asking too much!" Genesis 50:19–20; Job 23:8–10; 2 Corinthians 9:8.

4. You wonder, "Does God really know what's going on?" Isaiah 55:8–9; Matthew 6:8, 25–34; Romans 11:33–36.

5. You reason, "How could a loving God allow this to happen?" Psalm 73; Romans 8:28, 37–39; 2 Corinthians 12:7–10.

The truth is that you cannot determine or control how long you will have your husband, your children, your parents, your job, your home, or your health. If you'll release your emotional ownership of these things, you'll respond much more positively when the time comes to release back to Him what He so lovingly and willingly loaned you in the first place. And you'll be much more able to receive His comfort in your loss as well as thank Him for the time you had to enjoy His gifts.

Fruit in Due Season

I'll admit, it would be wonderful if we could see the fruit to come while the pruning is happening. But that's not how life in the vineyard works. Fruit takes time to mature. Pruning means we lose something now to gain something later—something we probably could never see or imagine at the moment.

That's why the Vinedresser invites us to trust Him. If you're in the middle of a painful pruning season right now, you may not even have the emotional energy to think, much less be grateful for what God is doing. But please know that our Father is patient and kind. He

You can pour out your heart and know that He cares—about your tomorrow and your today.

knows your heart, and His heart is broken with yours, too. Remember that He is the One who "heals the brokenhearted and binds up their wounds" (Psalm 147:3). His name is "the Father of mercies and God of all comfort" (2 Corinthians 1:3). You can pour out your heart and know that He cares—about your tomorrow and your today. His skillful hand is at work in your life accomplishing something in you that you could not do for yourself.

> *You'll be bearing more fruit for God—by your prayers, your choice to give thanks, and your daily actions before others.*

Make room in your heart for that miracle today. Give God the time He needs to accomplish something large and enduring and beautiful in your life for Him.

Whatever you do, don't let your resistance to God's pruning trip you into anger and rebellion. That will only send you back into a season of discipline—and God wants that even less for you than you do!

Instead, receive the gift from the Vinedresser's hand today and look forward, with confidence and anticipation, to the season of "more fruit" that is just around the corner. As soon as you do, you'll already be bearing more fruit for God—by your prayers, your choice to give thanks, and your daily actions before others. They'll see God's goodness affirmed by what you do and say in the midst of your circumstances. Your faith will plant the seeds of faith in them. They'll be encouraged, and God will be pleased and glorified.

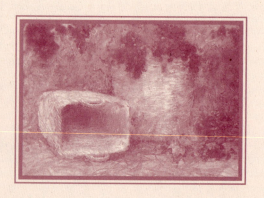

*"He who abides in Me,
and I in him, bears much fruit."*

JOHN 15:5

CHAPTER FIVE

The Miracle of Much Fruit

On the final day of harvest, the vineyard held its annual prize branch competition. The contest was based on a question the vinedresser had put to his workers when they first arrived: "Which single branch in my vineyard do you think will yield the most grapes?"

This year's results were astonishing. Entrants brought in heavier baskets than ever before. And the winner, to everyone's surprise, was a first-year worker—a young boy from Siena. He hauled in twenty more pounds of fruit from his one branch than the next closest contestant.

The young woman, at least, was suspicious.

"Papa," she asked as the last worker was departing, "how did that boy know which branch would win the prize?"

"He has a good memory."

"What do you mean?" she said.

"When he came here last winter to ask for a job, we walked

through the rows together." Her father winked. "I showed him which branch would win this year."

The daughter gasped in disbelief. "But how could you do that? The branches then were still completely bare!"

"Yes, but that's when you can see the place that will tell." He paused.

She waited, wanting him to say more, to explain what exactly he meant by the place that will tell.

"Come, I'll show you," her father said finally. They walked to a nearby row. "Look," he said, pointing to the place where a branch and vine met. "You measure the circumference of the branch here—do you see?—right where it comes out of the trunk."

Yes, she did see. The branch her father pointed to grew thick and strong out of the vine. She noticed that another branch nearby was only a quarter as big around at the same place.

Her father continued. "The size of this meeting place reveals the potential size of the harvest to come. The harvest cannot be greater than this union allows. It would be impossible! On the other hand, the greater this union, the greater can be the yield."

They looked over the rows of branches, clean-picked now until the next season. "And do you have more secrets that would win me a prize?" she asked.

"Perhaps," he said with a smile. "But none better."

The Miracle of Much Fruit

The biggest miracle in any vineyard is an unseen one. It flows like a silent river beneath the rough bark of the grape plant. It surges up through the trunk of the vine, out into the branches, and from there to the clusters of swelling fruit.

That unseen miracle is sap—the lifeblood of any vineyard. And as the vinedresser in our story knew, the greater the connection between branch and vine, the more lifeblood is available to produce fruit.

Of course, the power of sap to make an abundance of fruit matters most in a branch that is healthy (that isn't being dragged down by dirt and disease) and well-pruned (that isn't sending its nutrients in a dozen competing directions). Only then can the flow of life through the connecting place of vine to branch bring results that are truly miraculous.

Jesus' name for that mysterious and powerful connection is abiding. He said:

> *"He who abides in Me, and I in him, bears much fruit."*
>
> JOHN 15:5

What does Jesus mean by "abide"? It's not a word we use much these days, but the concept is simple. It means to stay, to remain, to continue in fellowship with. In that word, Jesus was calling His disciples to strengthen and enlarge their connection to Him, the Vine—to *be with Him* more and more.

And the direct result of such intimacy, Jesus promised, would be *"much fruit."*

If you think about the circumstances of that conversation in the vineyard, you can almost taste the anguish and the longing. After all, Jesus had just told His best friends that He was leaving. Physically, they would *not* be together! Yet He pleaded with them, *"Abide in Me, and I in you."* Within just six verses in John 15, you'll find that Jesus repeated His appeal to "abide" ten times!

So the first thing I want you to grasp in this chapter is just how much the Lord Jesus *wants* to abide with you. The Creator of the Universe, the perfect Son of God, the Savior of your soul wants to be in a continuing, growing, thriving, and incredibly productive relationship . . . with *you*.

> *You don't have to wait until you become more mature, more successful, or more accepted.*

You don't have to know more in order to abide. You don't have to wait until you become more mature, more successful, or more accepted. You don't have to prove yourself in any way more worthy. Right now, as you read this page, you are already the object of your Lord's attention and affection.

> *Stay with Me, He says.*
> *Be with Me.*
> *Remain in Me.*

Are you ready to hear that amazing invitation in a fresh way today? Then you may be ready to make a breakthrough to the most abundant life possible. And you'll find it in the third and final secret of the vine.

THE THIRD SECRET OF THE VINE:

If your life bears more fruit,
God will invite you to abide more deeply
with Him because that's how He produces
much fruit through you.

You might be as relieved as I was to learn that you don't reach your spiritual potential by cramming more serving or doing for God into your day! In fact, the opposite is true.

It's only as you pursue genuine and unbroken intimacy with Him that you can produce the most eternal fruit for His glory.

And that should be good news for any woman.

THE LANGUAGE OF WOMEN

Surely this last secret—abiding—is especially meaningful for us. Jesus is talking our language here, don't you think? It is the language of relationship, of mutual enjoyment, of personal connectedness. God seems to have gifted women with a special passion for closeness, both with those we love and with our Lord. Compared to the average male, most women I know seem to express their emotions more readily, enjoy fellowship more naturally, and desire togetherness more enthusiastically.

Can't you just feel the tension mounting in that little house?

But there's a catch.

God also seemed to wire us to care and tend and please more instinctively, too. And that often adds up to out-of-control demands and dawn-till-dusk busyness.

That's why abiding isn't automatic, even for us. We must choose, usually in the face of intense pressures, to heed the urgent call of Jesus to come away and "be with Me."

The familiar story of sisters Mary and Martha memorably portrays these competing priorities in our lives (Luke 10:38–42). When Jesus and His disciples stopped at their home in Bethany one day, "Mary . . . sat at Jesus' feet and heard His word. But Martha was distracted with much serving" (vv. 39–40).

Can't you just feel the tension mounting in that little house? Will it be *relationship* or will it be *service* that wins the day? Two sisters want to know!

Finally, a very agitated Martha asked Jesus to tell her sister to get up and start helping. But Jesus gave a tender and surprising reply:

> *"Martha, Martha, you are worried and troubled about many things. But one thing is needed, and Mary has chosen that good part."*
>
> VV. 41–42

Martha made the perfectly responsible "ministry" choice (I'm pretty sure I would have, too). She threw her energies and skills into making sure everything was going well and everyone was cared for. But Mary chose to abide with Jesus. And when Martha asked Jesus to rebuke her sister for not caring enough to serve Him, Jesus declined. Why? Because Mary had chosen to *be with Him*, and that was better than *doing for Him*.

Often I start my day as Mary. "Come be with Me," I hear the Lord saying. "In a moment, Lord," I reply. "But first I need to get a load of wash started, and Jessica ready, and I need to be out the door at . . ." Before I know it, the demands of the day have swept me away, worried and troubled about many things, and my name is Martha.

I sensed God asking me to spend the hour simply enjoying His presence.

Does this sound familiar to you? Most women I know struggle to get to the end of their to-do list each day. Spending time with God becomes just another activity on our list, when in fact it should be the paper on which we prioritize everything else we do!

God asks us to choose to abide, but look what happens when we don't. Jesus said:

> *"He who abides in Me, and I in him, bears much fruit; for without Me you can do nothing."*
> JOHN 15:5

Nothing? You and I tend to think that the only way to get more out of our day is to cram more into it. But the message of Jesus for us Martha's of the world is clear: *You're too busy not to abide!*

TOO BUSY *NOT* TO ABIDE

I happen to be a fairly organized person, and I enjoy being well prepared. For years I taught a monthly Bible study class, spending hours preparing my lessons and typing up handouts. But one month, a series of unexpected events kept me so busy that I couldn't prepare. The morning of class I finally got an hour to myself, but by then I was desperate. I knelt next to my bed and cried out to the Lord for His help. How did He want me to use that time?

> *I walked into class feeling stripped of the very things that usually gave me confidence.*

Strangely, I sensed God asking me to spend the hour simply enjoying His presence. So I took courage and stayed on my knees until it was time to go.

I walked into class feeling stripped of the very things that usually gave me confidence—organization, tools, a detailed plan. Since the normal schedule for class was out of the question, I opened in prayer, then turned to a favorite passage. From those treasured words, I talked about what

God had taught me over the years on that subject. As unplanned as the presentation was, not once during the lesson did I doubt that God was in it. I noticed women leaning forward listening, soaking up what was being shared. By the end of class, several were in tears. One woman wanted to know how I knew that my topic was the very issue she had been asking God to help her with.

As I drove home, I understood for the first time how doing less *for* God and being more *with* God produced *much* fruit. Now for you, that truth may seem obvious. But if you're one of my detail-oriented, super-organized sisters, I know you can understand what a breakthrough that was for me.

> *The busier we are, the more we need to abide.*

Let me share something else. The more experience we have in ministry, the easier it is to coast along on our talents, our store of knowledge, our experience, and our well-developed teaching aids . . . and leave God more and more out of the picture. Of course that's not our intention. But without being aware of it, we can forget that to do God's work, we need God's presence and power—and more of it all the time! In His invitation to abide, Jesus asks us to become more and more *dependent* on Him, and the amazing result is an abundance of fruit.

Think about it. Real and lasting fruit doesn't happen when you and I are not deeply connected to Jesus any more than a branch can bear fruit if it is lying on the ground. Jesus said:

> *"As the branch cannot bear fruit of itself, unless it abides in the vine, neither can you, unless you abide in Me."*
>
> v. 4

In fact, the busier we are, the more we need to abide. Because abiding is precisely how we are refueled and can avoid emotional and spiritual burnout.

So how does it work? And what do we have to do to abide?

That depends on who you are…

Every pilgrim travels toward God with a promise in hand—we can know God.

Tools to Abiding

Just as you relate to and communicate with each of your children differently, God invites each of us to abide with Him in our unique way. Yet all through Scripture and for thousands of years, the road to intimacy with God has had the same guideposts.

Being a pilgrim still requires humility, perseverance, obedience, and a genuine desire to know the Lord in a more personal way.

And every pilgrim travels toward God with a promise in hand—we *can* know God. "Draw near to God and He will draw near to you," the Bible says (James 4:8). "You will seek Me and find Me, when you search for Me with all your heart" (Jeremiah 29:13).

With this in mind, here are some suggestions that will help you begin or continue to abide.

My prayer seemed to go on forever. But when I opened my eyes, only five minutes had passed.

1. Make an appointment.

One morning while I was playing with my grandson, the doorbell rang. Jonathan was just a year old, so I picked him up and carried him to the door. The visitor was my neighbor dropping off a letter that had been left in her mailbox by mistake.

After we had chatted for several minutes, Jonathan put his little hands on each side of my face and turned it toward his. As I looked into his eyes, I realized he was saying, "Grandmother, I want all your attention."

That's what God wants from you. But that's difficult to

do unless you make a plan to abide, and make that plan a *priority*. Choose a time when you are at your best. Decide on a quiet and private place. Then make an appointment, write it down, and post it somewhere you can see it.

Keep it as regularly as you can. If you miss, apologize (just as you'd treat any best friend), and receive His forgiveness gratefully and confidently.

2. *Read and meditate on God's Letter to you.*

As a new Christian, reading my Bible was a spiritual discipline that helped me know what the Bible said and how God wanted me to live. But as I have grown in my faith, I have wanted more. I want to hear God's Word speaking directly into my life about pressing circumstances. More and more, I desire to have a personal encounter with Jesus on the pages of Scripture.

I believe this is what Jesus had in mind when He said, "Abide in Me." He wasn't advising His disciples to learn more about Jewish history or law; they already knew a lot about that. He was asking for an ongoing, personal encounter. Therefore, in your abiding time, I encourage you to read the Bible as God's letter to you. Let His words remain in you. Contemplate them. Take them with you from the room. Paul said, "Let the word of Christ dwell in you richly" (Colossians 3:16). And as you do, His words to you will begin to transform your thoughts and feelings and values.

3. Talk to God.

I remember the first time I determined to get up early and spend thirty minutes praying. It seemed simple enough. So I got down on my knees and prayed. I prayed for all my concerns, for everyone I could think of, and for everything around the world. My prayer seemed to go on forever. But when I opened my eyes, only five minutes had passed. *How do "spiritual" people pray for a whole hour?* I wondered.

The answer, I discovered, is that prayer is not a monologue, but a conversation with a friend. People who pray well talk to God well—as if He is there and listening and deeply involved, which He truly is.

It is helpful to have a list of people and situations that you pray for regularly (some things come up all the time between you and your other close friends, too). But because you're abiding with God Himself, you can also pour out your deepest fears, your hidden feelings, and your honest thoughts to Him. And of course, close friends also make a point of expressing their affection and gratitude often.

4. Keep a spiritual journal.

Write a letter to God each day in a notebook. This is not a diary of your day (although you may include some of that), but rather a record of how you are doing spiritually. Write down what God is teaching you. Record the Scriptures that mean the most to you. Write your prayers, and keep track of the answers. Ask and expect God to show you His heart, even as you write.

Don't give a second thought to how well you write or spell. Even the psalmist David knew, "Before a word is on my tongue you know it completely, O LORD" (Psalm 139:4, NIV). Your spiritual journal is private and personal. Go back to it often to see what God is doing in your life, and how you're changing.

5. Practice unbroken abiding.

Is it possible for a busy woman to be aware of God's presence every moment of every day—while you drive, shop, work, or even converse with another person? Everything else would be what you did *while* you were abiding with Christ.

The truth is that it *is* possible. Paul referred to it as "praying without ceasing." Brother Lawrence, a lay minister who spent years working in a monastery kitchen, called it "practicing the presence of God." It's easy for us to think of abiding as an event that ends when our quiet time ends. Then we go on with the real business of our day. But communing with the Lord is more like an ongoing attentiveness to the One who is *always* abiding with us. And we can do that anywhere.

A friend of mine describes unbroken abiding like this: "It's a silent conversation going on inside myself. But instead of thinking or talking to myself, I direct my thoughts toward God. He's always included. I'm learning to have a running conversation with Him no matter what I'm doing. My relationship has gone from a date I had with God in the morning to an all-day love affair in His presence."

My First Source

When you and I are deeply in touch with the source of all life, our lives change. Most of all, *we* change in important ways—and in very down-to-earth ways, too. Take your marriage or other primary relationships, for example.

I'll never forget how startled I was the day my new husband blurted out in some frustration, "It's not my job to make you happy."

"Then whose job is it?" I asked. But even before the words were out of my mouth I knew the answer. And it certainly wasn't my husband.

I'll admit that as a young wife I assumed that Bruce would be the ultimate source of fulfillment and happiness in my life (just like all the love songs promise). Yes, I loved God, and I wanted to grow in my faith. But the relationship I abided in most was with Bruce. That meant I looked to Bruce for the kind of intimacy that would make me feel whole, significant, and content. When Bruce failed to deliver at this impossible task, I could become desperate and demanding.

Does this pattern sound familiar to you? When a woman makes someone other than Jesus the ultimate source of her contentment, she ends up taxing others unreasonably, asking them to meet spiritual and emotional needs that can only be met by God. The results can be painful and disillusioning.

> *You will tend to ask for the very things that are His will and delight to give.*

God may proactively prune us in this area, causing others to *withhold* what we want from them because He wants us to receive it from Him. Remember that our God describes Himself as a jealous God (Exodus 34:14). He asks to be our first affection, our first provider, our first security.

Perhaps you haven't heard the "jealousy" in these words from Jesus to you about abiding:

> *"As the Father loved Me, I also have loved you; abide in My love."*
> JOHN 15:9

As you abide in this wonderful, attentive, and fulfilling love of God, you can expect other relationships in your life to improve dramatically! They don't have to fill you up—God does. They don't have to explain and sustain your existence—God does. I don't mean that human relationships will lose their importance in your life. But instead of allowing your needs to define and limit those relationships, you will more often come to them brimming with the love of God, ready to give freely from the river of abundance that flows from His heart through yours.

Let me show you in more detail how that will happen.

GRAPE EXPECTATIONS

The power of abiding in a woman's life will change you from the inside out:

You will become more like Christ.

As you spend more and more time being with Him, you'll notice the character of Jesus being developed in you. It's a fact that the more time you spend with a person, the more you take on their traits. Spend time in the gospels and make a list of some of the qualities of Jesus you would like to be true of you. Then watch God produce them in you as you abide in Him more frequently.

You will gain wisdom and discernment.

The more time you spend with God, the more you'll grow in godly discernment. God wants you to know His will, and He will give you wisdom as you wait patiently on Him (James 1:5).

When you need to make an important decision—abide. God will faithfully direct you as you spend time in His presence. When you are struggling with a relationship—abide. When you are uncertain about whether you are being pruned or disciplined—abide. God will be faithful to reveal the truth to you.

You will pray more in keeping with God's will—and He will answer.

Jesus said, "If you abide in Me, and My words abide in you, you will ask what you desire, and it shall be done for you" (John 15:7). What an astonishing promise! Yet it makes sense. When you are abiding deeply in Jesus, your heart and mind become much more attuned to Him and His purposes. As a result, you will tend to ask for the very things that are His will and delight to give.

You will experience His peace and presence.

The more time you spend with Christ, the more you will experience the peace of His presence even in the midst of trials and crisis. A friend of mine recently found herself caught in the middle of a robbery in progress. She was tempted to run for the exit sign, but clearly sensed God saying, "Don't run!"

> *He wants the pleasure of your company—anytime, anywhere, anyhow.*

"After the ordeal was over," she says, "I realized that I had been calm throughout it. And had I run for the door, I may have been shot. I believe I heard God because my heart was at peace, and that has come from the disciplines of abiding in my life. I'm learning to believe that safety doesn't exist in the absence of danger, but in the presence of God."

And besides all this, the practice of abiding will bring you a special and very personal gift from Jesus. He called it "My joy."

Five Abiding Busters

adapted from *Secrets of the Vine Bible Study*

See if you recognize yourself in the "abiding busters" on this page (each example, while powerful, is wrong). Let the Bible help you discover a new breakthrough truth, and write it down (in your own words) in your journal.

1. The "But I Don't Feel Anything" Foul-Up. *You assume if you didn't have strong emotions, nothing happened.* Psalm 145:18; 1 John 3:19–20.

2. The "He Doesn't Like Me" Muddle. *You believe God loves you, but you doubt that He actually likes you.* John 15:15; Ephesians 3:17–19; 1 John 3:1.

3. The "I'm Too Busy" Blunder. *You let your schedule keep you from regular abiding, but you think God will connect with you anyway.* Isaiah 40:31; Matthew 6:33; Matthew 11:28.

4. The "Sin Doesn't Matter" Mistake. *You think ongoing disobedience won't keep you from abiding, especially if you experience pleasant feelings during church.* Psalm 15; Psalm 66:18–20; James 4:8; 1 John 1:5-7.

5. The "Going Through the Motions" Notion. *You think Bible reading and prayer are proof you're having a relationship with God.* 1 Samuel 16:7; Psalm 27:4–8; Matthew 5:6.

An Invitation to Joy

Joy, you see, was ultimately the very reason Jesus gave for His message in the vineyard. He said so Himself:

> *"These things I have spoken to you, that My joy may remain in you, and that your joy may be full."*
>
> V. 11

You might be a mother of a newborn who has you up all hours of the night. You might be caring almost hourly for an elderly and ailing parent. You might feel completely unable or unworthy to sit at Jesus' feet.

If you say yes, He will give you His joy.

Jesus wants you to know the truth today. He wants the pleasure of your company—anytime, anywhere, anyhow—and if you say yes, He will give you His joy.

I hope that these past few chapters have stirred in you an increasing desire for extraordinary fruitfulness for God. In our next and final chapter, we're going to ask some key questions about your relationship with your Father. Together, we'll uncover potential barriers that would keep you from experiencing all He has in mind for your life.

Remember, what God has in mind for you is so far beyond what you are experiencing right now that you can't possibly imagine it. You—one magnificent branch in the Father's vineyard—were made for abundance.

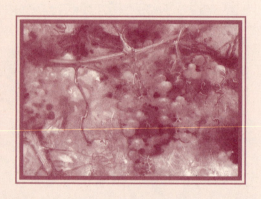

*He who has begun
a good work in you will complete it
until the day of Jesus Christ.*

PHILIPPIANS 1:6

CHAPTER SIX

Your Father's Prize

She sat by the window of the train watching the red tile roofs, hilltop villages, and neatly tended vineyards of Tuscany slip past. Siena, Empoli, Pontedera . . . the valley towns of her childhood memory came and went. Soon the train would turn north, taking her away from Italy and back to her life in the city.

Suddenly she remembered her father's parting gift. She pulled the little package from her coat pocket, and when she opened it, an oval silver locket fell into her lap.

She examined it, delighted. On its cover, the locket showed an embossing of a grape cluster. Inside it held a sepia photograph. The picture showed her as a small girl sitting astride her father's broad shoulders as he stood proudly beside a row of his beloved grapes.

On the facing frame she read in tiny script, "You will always be my greatest prize. Love, Papa."

At that moment, a thought occurred to her. Why it hadn't before, she couldn't say. What she saw for the first time was that her father's prize-winning ways with a vineyard were like a picture of how he had always cared for her.

Gazing out the window, she thought about his dedication to a lifetime of coaxing a harvest from his grapes. And how, with an even greater dedication, he had coaxed an abundance of the heart from her life—gently correcting her when necessary, firmly guiding her toward maturity, and consistently proving his unconditional love.

As the train clattered toward the border, her future seemed to rush toward her, faster and faster. But the future she saw was full of promise. Her father had prepared her for whatever lay ahead. And holding the picture of it tightly in her hands, she basked in the glow of joyful anticipation.

I trust that our time in the vineyard together has been a refreshing and encouraging experience for you. My prayer is that, as you leave these pages, you'll take with you a new portrait of your heavenly Father's love, along with a deeper desire to cooperate with His ways in your life.

Jesus said, "My Father is always at his work . . . and I, too, am working" (John 5:17, NIV). Isn't that amazing? God Himself is at work—always—in every circumstance of our life, and in every challenge we face!

And how kind it is of Jesus to give us such a memorable illustration of this miracle! A vine. A branch full of promise. A Vinedresser, always at work. A plan for a huge harvest from every disciple . . .

Yet the truth is that many women do not reach for the promise. They hesitate here, at the threshold of spiritual and emotional abundance. Why? Sooner or later, it seems to me, the issue reveals itself to be a relational one—a basic question of trust between daughter and Father.

I think of a Vermont woman named Maeve. After reading *Secrets of the Vine*, she called it a "volume of hope." It had helped her to resolve a long-standing break in her relationship with her Father. "I always felt like God's stepdaughter," she wrote. "Even though I was saved at eighteen, I have often felt emotionally destitute. Personal challenges in my life and years of physical suffering had convinced me that I was an unloved stepchild of my heavenly Father. But now I see that I misunderstood Him completely."

> Hundreds of women I've met live under the shadow of an "unpleasable" heavenly Father.

How would you describe your relationship with your Father? Is something still keeping you from reaching for what God wants to give you?

As we close this little book, ask the Holy Spirit to show you what unfinished business there might be between you and the Father. Ask Him to reveal anything that might be holding you back from responding wholeheartedly to His hand in your life.

You may be just one step away from the breakthrough you've wanted for years.

THE PLEASURE OF YOUR COMPANY

Sharon, another *Secrets* reader, wrote to say that she was struck with the statement that many Christians don't really believe God likes them. "How sad, and how true!" she wrote. "I see God as Someone who must be constantly disappointed in me, who is 'unpleasable,' instead of someone who really enjoys my company."

Sharon isn't alone. Hundreds of women I've met live under the shadow of an "unpleasable" heavenly Father. Whatever they might sing or say in church, these women go home to a God they believe is untrustworthy and unlikable. Yes, they believe God *loves* them—loving the world is His job, after all. But *like?* A Father who wants to be close to them *every minute of the day?* Impossible to imagine!

You can see how this common "heartsickness" would leave a Christian woman extremely reluctant to let the

Vinedresser anywhere near the branch of her life.

Do you believe in a God who really would enjoy the pleasure of your company? It's time to find out.

Bruce often uses a simple diagnostic chart that I've found helpful. It presents a series of words that describe God's attitude or feeling toward you. You mark the point on the scale that seems most accurate for you. Don't respond according to what you may have been taught. Respond according to how you honestly think and feel most of the time!

I think of God as:

STINGY — **GENEROUS**
1 2 3 4 5 6 7 8 9 10

HARSH — **MERCIFUL**
1 2 3 4 5 6 7 8 9 10

UNINTERESTED — **ATTENTIVE**
1 2 3 4 5 6 7 8 9 10

SHORT-TEMPERED — **PATIENT**
1 2 3 4 5 6 7 8 9 10

On which side of the scale do your choices fall? If your answers are lined up far to the right, you have an accurate picture of God. If your answers line up on the left, you probably identify with Sharon—which means that trusting the hand of the Vinedresser in your life will continue to seem impossible.

Let's look at a major common barrier in each season of a woman's life in the vineyard.

Fear of the Father

Your greatest barrier to responding to God's discipline for ongoing sin might be fear. You might say, "Even if what I'm doing is wrong, I'm afraid to face God. What if He hurts me?"

The idea of fatherly discipline may have become emotionally tangled with chaos, violence, abuse, and neglect.

This response often stems from a negative experience with your own father or other father figure. "My father's idea of discipline," says Louise, "was to tell me I was ugly, fat, and no one would every marry me." Marli says, "Mostly I remember my stepdad's drunken rages and getting slapped so hard I flew across the room."

Sometimes a woman's response isn't so much fear as

emptiness. After Tami's mother left her father and moved across the country, her life changed radically. "My dad pretty much let me run wild," she said. "I don't think he really cared." Many others grow up in homes where a father is largely absent. *Father* becomes just another word for rejection and loss.

If you've had similar experiences growing up, the idea of fatherly discipline may have become emotionally tangled with chaos, violence, abuse, and neglect.

But our heavenly Father is different! Even in Bible times, the comparisons between earthly and heavenly father needed a little clarification. The writer of Hebrews contrasted the imperfect discipline of our earthly fathers, who could only do "as they thought best" with the life-giving discipline of God, which is "for our good" (Hebrews 12:10, NIV).

To let go of your old, broken idea of "father" and reach for a new one, you will need to open your heart to a healing truth: God is the perfect Father. Every time He intervenes in your life, His intention is to free you from a destructive choice that will take you in the wrong direction and away from Him. His actions are loving, tender, and wise—and the results are life giving.

That's why the Bible tells us never to despise or reject God's hand of discipline. Instead, we should "readily be in subjection to the Father of spirits *and live*" (Hebrews 12:9, emphasis added).

Consider these important truths about God's discipline:

- *Your heavenly Father's methods are perfect.* He never abuses His children. He's never too harsh or too lenient. He doesn't lose His temper. Exodus 34:6–7; Deuteronomy 1:30–31; Psalm 34.

- *Your heavenly Father's motives are perfect.* He is not trying to punish you or "even the score." He receives no personal satisfaction when He disciplines His "kids." Jeremiah 29:11; Ephesians 2:4–7; James 1:17.

- *Your heavenly Father's commitment is perfect.* He will actively pursue you, yet He honors your freedom of choice. What He wants most for you is what will bring you lasting fulfillment. Psalm 138; 1 Corinthians 1:26–29; 2 Peter 1:4.

- *Your heavenly Father's love for you is unconditional.* Your Father doesn't love you less because you're struggling with ongoing sin. He doesn't *like* you any less, either. His love for you is unending. Psalm 86:5; 2 Corinthians 1:3; 1 John 3:1.

If this is an area where you struggle, I encourage you to spend time with the Scriptures listed here. When you are ready, take the steps your Father is waiting for: Tell Him you will trust Him with your life, repent sincerely of the sin and misunderstandings that have kept you apart, and turn wholeheartedly in submission to Him. You can expect God to begin a beautiful healing process in your heart.

He has only a wonderful, fruitful future in mind for you, His precious child.

Resistance to His plan

A woman told me recently, "I would prefer to always be changed through pleasant and enjoyable circumstances." I understood her immediately, and I'm sure you do, too!

The most common barrier in pruning for women might be expressed like this: "Pruning feels too much like losing something important to me, *and I can't seem to let go.*"

Let that activity or attachment or possession go—He has something much better in mind for you.

If you're fearful or resistant about something God is trying to change in your life today, you will benefit from taking many of the same steps of trust I outlined for discipline in the previous section.

Even though you're not involved in an ongoing sin issue, your relationship with God is still hindered by your lack of trust in Him. And it takes trust—plus plenty of courage—to let go.

Yet the Bible says, "The works of His hands are faithful and just; all His precepts are trustworthy" (Psalm 111:7, NIV). "You are good, and what you do is good; teach me your decrees" (Psalm 119:68, NIV).

The breakthrough that's waiting for you is to choose to believe and act on a fundamental truth: *Your Father is good.* He is all-wise, all-loving, and all-powerful, and He is at work in you to redirect your energies toward a much more fruit-filled future than you can see at the moment.

We need to let go of a reliance on an emotional experience to prove to us that God is real or that He loves us.

With you specifically in mind, He has considered all the options, determined the most important area to focus on, and chosen the perfect time and method. That's what it means to be a perfect Father. And that's why you can trust Him enough to surrender to His pruning. So let that activity or attachment or possession go—He has something much better in mind for you. Accept the difficult time or season of suffering—God is in control, and He's at work in you for your *good.*

The same woman who confessed to wishing that God would bring only pleasant circumstances into our lives went on to say: "Of course, the lessons I've learned through the difficult times can't be compared with those I learned when everything was easy—if I learned anything at all. God has used tests of faith to get my preoccupation off of myself, and then He is able to show me more of Himself."

FREEDOM ABOUT FEELINGS

If abiding is the secret to the most spiritual abundance possible, and the only way to experience the deepest levels of intimacy with God, why do so few of us seem to succeed at it?

Based on what I've heard from Christian women over the years, I've concluded that one of the most common barriers to abiding could be described like this: *If I don't feel anything, nothing must be happening.*

Feelings do matter. God created you with emotions, and He cares about your heart. But if you assume abiding always brings with it a warm rush of feelings, then when you feel little or nothing, you'll decide you're not abiding. Soon you'll lose interest. Eventually, rather than deal with feelings of guilt and failure, you may give up altogether.

We all know, though, that emotional responses are determined by many factors—our physical condition, how much sleep we've had, whether we're anxious or depressed, how well we're getting along with our husband, whether we've had our morning coffee, the weather, our basic temperament type . . . it's a long list! And we don't judge our marriages or other significant friendships by feelings alone on any given day.

No wonder gauging intimacy with God by our emotions only eventually gets us in trouble.

Thankfully, emotion is a wonderful part of a genuine spiritual experience. Those feelings of exhilaration and release are God's gifts to us, and they inspire us to love Him more. Yet to grow toward maturity, we need to let go of a reliance on an emotional experience to prove to us that God is real or that He loves us.

The abiding breakthrough I invite you to make is to vow to pursue God in a sincere, respectful friendship for the rest of your life *no matter what you feel*. No other relationship could be as important, and none will ultimately be as fulfilling.

Every day, Jesus gives you an invitation: "Behold, I stand at the door and knock. If anyone hears My voice and opens the door, I will come in to him and dine with him, and he with Me" (Revelation 3:20).

Do you want Him to come in for a visit? Then keep opening that door every day of your life.

CHOSEN FOR GLORY

Did you know that grape plantings in California's Napa Valley often don't reach peak productivity for fifty years? Fruitfulness takes time. And overflowing abundance for God usually takes a lifetime.

But now you know that God *is* at work in you today! And you can be absolutely confident of this—"that He who has begun a good work in you will complete it until the day of Jesus Christ" (Philippians 1:6).

So no matter what season of life you're in today, be encouraged. Your future in God is a thing of beauty. And He is taking great delight in watching you grow.

Of course, on that day—not far from now—when you stand before Jesus with the fruit of your life, you probably won't see a single grape! Instead, you'll see faces. Your "fruit" will crowd around you with joy and celebration. In those faces you'll see your spouse, children, coworkers, family members, and neighbors you took one step closer to Christ. You'll see people around the world you haven't even met yet who were impacted by the commitments you made today.

> *When you stand before Jesus with the fruit of your life, you probably won't see a single grape! Instead, you'll see faces.*

You could see people God will bring into your path one hour from now!

On that day, when the Father looks at you and says, "Well done, good and faithful servant!" you'll know that your passion to bear fruit for His glory was the best decision you ever made as a child of God.

Take these vineyard teachings of Jesus with you in the very center of your heart as you continue your spiritual journey. Remember, you are loved unconditionally. You are being led each day into greater fulfillment and purpose for Him. And you have been chosen for abundance.

May your basket overflow!

Appendix

THREE SEASONS IN GOD'S VINEYARD

Distinctive Issues	THE SEASON OF DISCIPLINE	THE SEASON OF PRUNING	THE SEASON OF ABIDING
YOUR MAIN ARENA OF GROWTH	Sin	Self	Savior
GOD'S MAIN OBJECTIVE FOR YOU	Purify your behavior	Prioritize your values	Pursue your relationship with Him
WHAT GOD WANTS MOST FROM YOU	Obedience—to stop your sinning	Trust—to drop your distractions	Love—to deepen your friendship
WHAT YOUR BEST RESPONSE WOULD BE	Repentance	Relinquishment	Relationship
WHAT YOU SHOULD SAY WHEN YOU PRAY	"Help me, Lord! Forgive me and deliver me from sin."	"Use me, Lord! Change me so I can do more for you."	"Draw me closer to You, Lord! Nothing else really matters but You!"
WHAT YOU WILL EXPERIENCE	Restoration	Release	Rest
WHEN THIS SEASON WILL END	It ends when you stop the sin	It ends when you change your priorities	It doesn't have to end (God wants it to go on forever!)
WHAT GOD WANTS MOST TO GIVE YOU	Fruit from an obedient life	More fruit from a pruned life	Much fruit from an abiding life

PRAYER WITH A FEMININE EDGE
Ask for Extravagant Blessing

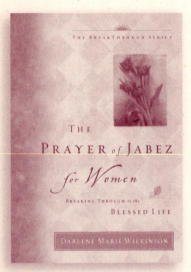

The phenomenal impact of *The Prayer of Jabez* is shown by reports of changed lives, expanded ministries, and spiritual breakthroughs among believers everywhere. Now women have their own unique version, written by Bruce Wilkinson's lifetime partner in marriage, that is full of significance for women's roles and ministry opportunities in God's kingdom. A must-read for every woman, whether she has read *The Prayer of Jabez* or not, this book addresses important questions, such as, *How can a busy mom expand her territory without neglecting the most important territory she already has, her family?* Darlene Marie Wilkinson's warm, personable approach reaches out to her reader, encouraging her to become like Jabez and experience the extraordinary life.

ISBN 1-57673-962-7

- The Prayer of Jabez for Women Audiocassette   ISBN 1-57673-963-
- The Prayer of Jabez   ISBN 1-57673-733-0
- The Prayer of Jabez Audiocassette   ISBN 1-57673-842-6
- The Prayer of Jabez Audio CD   ISBN 1-57673-907-
- The Prayer of Jabez Leather Edition   ISBN 1-57673-857-
- The Prayer of Jabez Journal   ISBN 1-57673-860-
- The Prayer of Jabez Devotional   ISBN 1-57673-844-
- The Prayer of Jabez Bible Study   ISBN 1-57673-979-
- The Prayer of Jabez Bible Study: Leader's Edition   ISBN 1-57673-980-
- The Prayer of Jabez Gift Edition   ISBN 1-57673-810-
- The Prayer of Jabez for Teens   ISBN 1-57673-815-
- The Prayer of Jabez for Teens Audio CD   ISBN 1-57673-904-